Crystal Lee

Crystal Lee

A Woman of Inheritance

HENRY P. LEIFERMANN

MACMILLAN PUBLISHING CO., INC.

NEW YORK

Macmillan Publishing Co., Inc.
866 Third Avenue, New York, N.Y. 10022
Collier Macmillan Canada, Ltd.

Library of Congress Cataloging in Publication Data

Leifermann, Henry P
Crystal Lee : a woman of inheritance.

1. Jordan, Crystal Lee, 1940–
2. Textile workers—North Carolina. 3. Trade-unions—North Carolina. 4. Cotton Trade—North Carolina.
I. Title.
HD8073.J65L44 331.88′17′700924 [B]
75-14118
ISBN 0-02-570220-3

First Printing 1975

Printed in the United States of America

FOR

NANCY

ACKNOWLEDGMENTS

MANY PERSONS IN Roanoke Rapids and elsewhere in North Carolina, in numerous interviews conducted over a considerable period of time, helped provide the material for this book. Among them were members and employes of the Textile Workers Union of America and employes of J. P. Stevens & Company, Inc.

Portions of Crystal Lee Jordan's story first appeared in different form, in *The New York Times Magazine*, whose editors, particularly Gerald Walker, I thank.

For their patient cooperation and specific contributions I wish to thank Crystal Lee Jordan, Larry Jordan, Jr., Eli Zivkovich, and their relatives and friends.

I especially thank Amanda Vaill for her encouragement and judgment in editing this book.

H. P. L.

"According to the tribes of your fathers ye shall inherit."

—The Book of Numbers

1

BOTH THE GIRL and the man felt the bond between them. They never spoke of it to each other, but now, riding in the car, just before dark, the girl wondered about it—how it could seem to be kindness, support of each other, and still make each one hostage to the other; how it could put the two of them apart from the rest of the family. The girl, Crystal Lee Pulley, was fourteen, and she could not remember when this tie with the man, her father, had not existed; it was always just there.

It was nearly eight o'clock at night, dusk. The sun would not fully set for at least another half-hour. The heat of an August day in the South came out of the ground, sucked up from dry pine forests, from peanut fields, off the broad leaves of tobacco plants, up from rows of cotton, drawn from the earth as though dusk were a sponge.

Crystal Lee, sitting in the back seat of the car next to her brother, Bobby Wayne, and her sister, Geraldine, noticed only the heat making layers and waves on the highway. Her face pointed toward fields flowing by the car, and her eyes held an unfocused stare.

It was August 1955, and the Pulley family was moving. Crystal Lee was excited about it, about the strangeness of moving a family. There was nothing she could think of back in Roanoke Rapids that she would miss more than a day or two. Even missing Gilbert Newsome, her boy friend, would not be any different in their new home than it was in Roanoke Rapids, because he was away in the Army now. There would be letters from Gilbert. There were letters before.

Albert Pulley drove the car easily, one hand on the wheel and one hand resting on the front seat between him and his wife, Odell. He knew the highway well and had made the drive from Roanoke Rapids to Burlington, from eastern North Carolina to central North Carolina, several times that month, looking for work in the cotton mills of Burlington and in the small mill towns nearby, Haw River and Glen Raven. Now he and his family, with the exception of his seventeen-year-old married daughter, Syretha, were leaving Roanoke Rapids and the cotton mills there, going to Burlington and the cotton mills there. To an outsider, this change in towns and jobs might seem hardly a change at all. The physical differences between the two towns, and the mills, and the kind of work to be found at either place, were slight. The distance from one to the other is not great—only 135 miles. But Albert Pulley had great and complex expectations of the changes this move would bring to his life and to his family.

Pulley was a big man, more than six feet tall. He had a handsome face, although he constantly had to watch his weight, and every month or two the family bore with him through one diet or another. His daughter, Crystal Lee, thought him the handsomest man she knew. And Albert Pulley thought Crystal Lee, with her long dark-brown hair and pale-green eyes, was turning out to be as pretty, or prettier than, his wife. He noticed too, with some discomfort, his daughter's skin, cool and white as milk in a pitcher, and the fresh, bursting figure she was already acquiring. He would have to watch her closely in Burlington.

Roanoke Rapids, in the last of his months there, was a sour town for Albert Pulley. He was a loom fixer in the cotton mill, and as good as any mechanic he knew, able to see or sense what caused a loom to stop weaving: a jammed shuttle no longer flying back and forth over the threads, a bobbin no longer reeling off yarn. As he roamed the plank floors of the weave room, it was usually only a moment from the time he heard a weaver's shout until he slipped between the looms, gauging the stopped machine like a target he had spotted, pulling a wrench from his toolbox as he went, then, bent over the loom, making one adjustment or another, then stepping back to watch it start again, to listen to the click-clack of the wood shuttle and the smash of old wheels and gears lifting and pulling the loom. He was at his best and fastest when he heard his wife's call on the weave-room floor. Weavers held their jobs only on the measurement of how much cloth they could turn out of a loom, and a stopped loom meant a drop in that day's wages for Odell Pulley.

In his last months in Roanoke Rapids, Albert Pulley had begun to hope for more than loom-fixing. He took a trade-school course in textiles on his own time because his bossman told him they both could expect promotions soon, the bossman to another shift, Pulley to the bossman's job. Pulley talked with the family about it, and they began to count on the promotion because of his expectations, just as he counted on it because of the bossman's talk. But that had been all it was—talk. The bossman argued with a higher supervisor, was told to find work elsewhere, did so, and Albert Pulley was not promoted. As far as Crystal Lee knew, that was the only time in his life Albert Pulley ever tried to be more, ever expected to become more than a mill hand.

Years later, remembering the move to Burlington, Crystal Lee said, "My daddy's brother, Dick, he's the bossman now. He was the only one in my daddy's family to finish school, but he wasn't any smarter than my daddy. Only thing was, maybe, he didn't drink. He was very quiet, while my daddy, he'd fight in a minute if somebody said something he didn't like. He'd lay 'em out, you know? That's probably why Dick got a bossman's job, and Daddy never did. Though he had worked. He was really trying, and then it all fell in on him."

In the late summer of 1955, however, the Pulleys, especially Albert and Crystal Lee, felt a change might lead to better things. Albert Pulley sold the family's old frame house in Roanoke Rapids to his sister and her husband, collecting much of his equity in a television set the brother-in-law included in the deal. It was the first set the Pulleys had had. "I remember how excited I was to think that we were going to move. I remember thinking how different, exciting maybe, it was going to be. You know, maybe a chance to just start over, meet new people; that things would be so much better," Crystal Lee says now. Most of the Pulleys' possessions went ahead of them in a Red Ball Lines moving van. There were small boxes on the floor of the car, some toys, Odell Pulley's favorite vases that she would not trust to moving men, blankets and pillows for them all. Albert Pulley had said they might sleep awhile on the side of the road that night, because of the late start and his already tiring day—he had already made one journey that day from Burlington, where he had started working, back to Roanoke Rapids to pick up his family.

It was the family's pattern, set by Odell Pulley, to be as cautious as possible with Albert Pulley in times like this. He tried to control every part of his life, and of theirs, but often there was little that he did control. The past spring, when Bobby Pulley had been dating a bossman's daughter, walking her home from high school and going to her family's house, Albert Pulley had had to be quiet and take a tongue-lashing. The girl's father came to the Pulleys' house one night. He said Bobby was not good enough for his daughter. He wanted Albert Pulley to keep his son away from the girl. "I remember the feeling that gave me, because I could imagine the feeling that it gave my father. And yet, my father had to work in the cotton mill, and all he could do was stop his son from coming to see this man's daughter, or possibly lose his job. My mother's too," Crystal Lee says. Odell Pulley told the children never to mention it around Albert.

The Pulleys' first home in Roanoke Rapids was a graying wood-frame duplex at 316B Monroe Street, a short walk from Albert Pulley's job at Roanoke Mill #2. Odell Pulley's parents lived with them, and the four children and four adults filled every corner in their half of the small house. The mill owned the house. The mill owned every other house in town, each house the same distance from its neighbors and the same distance from its street, each street drawn straight in a pattern of blocks set by the mill. It was only a few blocks' walk from the Pulleys' house to the small hospital, the only one in town (it, too, was owned by the mill), where Crystal Lee was born on the last day of 1940.

By the time Crystal Lee was in the second grade, the Pulleys had stepped up from the duplex to a house at 309 Henry Street, four blocks from the cotton mill—they rented this house from the mill too. It was a "shotgun house"—its long, narrow hallway ran the depth of the house, from front door to back, with all the rooms off one side or the other of this hallway. A man could fire down the hallway with a shotgun, the charge going in the front door and out the back, and not hit a thing: a shotgun house. In the back yard was a small chicken coop. One night Albert Pulley came home with several young hens, barely more than chicks, and announced to his family that soon they would have all the fresh eggs, and hens, they would want. That first week the young hens were kept in the bathroom while Albert Pulley repaired the chicken coop. For weeks he fed his chickens every day before leaving for the mill. Finally, one night, after the hens had reached egg-laying and fryer size, someone stole the entire roost. Albert Pulley did not replace the stolen chickens. He gave up on the idea and turned the coop into a playhouse, used mostly by Crystal Lee.

There in the coop, with the great seriousness of very young children who are pretending to be older than they are, Crystal Lee enrolled her neighborhood friends in school. Albert Pulley found a piece of blackboard for her, and Crystal Lee, being the effective owner of the coop, played teacher to her friends' students. At night, in bed but not asleep, she drew and redrew plans, decors, furniture arrangements for the school. Most days, playing in the yard, she layered herself with dust and dirt, and she had to learn to judge how soon her mother or father would be home from the mill. Just before they arrived, she would fill a pan with water and scrub away most of the grime. Some summer afternoons her daddy let her sit naked in a heavy steel washtub in the back yard, and he poured cold water over her while she laughed and splashed.

His family called Albert Pulley "Little Fella," because he wasn't. There was a time when he took that kind of joke with an open, laughing face. Odell Pulley, who had not worked long in the cotton mills then, was a pretty woman. "She had coal-black hair," Crystal Lee remembers. "It never got as long as mine, but it was long. And always on payday, I don't remember whether it was on Thursday or Friday, but she'd always come home and take a bath and fix her hair." Odell Pulley was a quiet woman, and she seemed sad in contrast with her open, laughing husband. The day she got her first job in the cotton mills, in Roanoke #2 where Albert worked, she cried. "She cried because she was happy in a way. She needed the job, we needed the money," Crystal Lee says. But Odell Pulley did not let her husband see her tears.

Albert Pulley loved to cook. On holidays he cooked two or three different meats, ham, chicken and beef, boiling them in a large wash pot, and Odell baked cakes for the visiting Pulley kin. Odell's family rarely visited them, not because of any estrangement between the families, but because her relatives kept to themselves. Even when her parents had lived with Albert and Odell, they had kept to themselves except at mealtimes. What her parents called home in the Henry Street house was a back room that had a bed, two chairs, a table, and a chest of drawers, and they used a sink on the back porch.

Odell Pulley's side of the family was not unique in its reclusiveness. In small cotton-mill towns—and Roanoke Rapids has about 14,000 residents—the mill hands and their families do not often gather together unless it is to listen to a preacher's vision of the heaven or hell that awaits them, or to go to work in the mills. So a group seen in high spirits, eating, drinking corn liquor or store whiskey, swapping gossip and tales, is assumed to be all family, counted in degrees of cousins, aunts and uncles.

Odell and Albert Pulley generally were happy with each other. There were more arguments between the two than Crystal Lee could count, but that was always marked down to Albert Pulley's quick temper, which the children and his wife accepted and expected, and to his occasional drinking spells, a matter that Odell Pulley, who rarely drank liquor, bore in pain. There was no doubt the couple loved each other. And there was no question that Albert Pulley was the complete master at home. "If we wanted to go somewhere, I'd go ask Momma first. She'd say you gotta go ask your daddy. I always had to have Daddy's permission. If I didn't have Daddy's permission, I didn't go nowhere," Crystal Lee says. If that arrangement upset Odell Pulley, she never showed it. "Daddy was the type of man, he liked to have a good time. He loved people. Momma was more of a loner, like. As long as she just had Daddy, she was satisfied."

For many years, Albert and Odell Pulley worked together on the first shift at the cotton mill. They had to be at the gates by seven in the morning and work until three in the afternoon. They rose early to get the children, Crystal Lee, Bobby, Geraldine and Syretha, ready for grade school. Then the parents would leave, and an hour later, the children would set out across the railroad tracks that lay between Henry Street and the school. Many mornings Crystal Lee and Bobby had to duck under the car couplings of a parked freight train in order to get there. Crystal Lee didn't mind. Partly because her brother was the closest to her age in the family, and partly because she preferred the company and the ways of boys to girls, she had become a tomboy. She had inherited her father's quick temper, and she often had to count on the nearby presence of Bobby to back up her fights. She gave a stiff beating to her best girl friend once, because the girl had told Albert Pulley about a spanking Crystal Lee got in school. She could take punishment too. In the sixth grade, when she was playing baseball and was hit in the eye by a fly ball, Crystal Lee refused to cry. She and her father laughed about it, and Albert Pulley doctored the eye.

The Pulleys lived a routine. Every payday, after she bathed and fixed her hair, Odell Pulley led her four children uptown to buy groceries and pay the week's bills. On Saturdays, if they did not have to work, Albert and Odell took their children shopping —that is, the four children stayed in the car while their parents went in the stores. In summer, during the week of July Fourth, the mills shut down to give the workers a one-week vacation. The Pulleys always drove to the beach, usually Virginia Beach near Norfolk, or the Outer Banks near Nags Head. Odell Pulley did not like to see her children swim in the ocean. But Crystal Lee usually slipped away to go fishing with her father—just the two of them—and on those side-trips, Albert Pulley could be counted on to say, "Honey, I can't help it if you fall in," and Crystal Lee always managed to "fall in" and go swimming.

The Pulleys' life was not much different from the days and weeks, winters and summers, of every other family on Henry Street, and on Monroe Street before then, and on Jefferson Street, their third and last address in Roanoke Rapids. All of their friends and neighbors were mill hands too. "I never cared where children's parents worked at," Crystal Lee says. "It never dawned on me, up until I was in sixth grade. That's when I was old enough to realize there was a difference. The sixth grade was a school just for sixth-graders, so we were brought in from all the elementary schools. I was throwed in with the doctors' children, and the lawyers' children, and I realized that there was a difference: that the doctors' children and the lawyers' children stayed together, and the poor children were left in a classroom all by themselves, and I was one of the poor children." She came to believe, eventually, that "well, maybe they are better than me."

Albert Pulley was his own amateur mechanic, tuning the Dodge sedan himself, caring for the car the way a man will when he has few possessions and finds those he does have to be rich and surprising. The August night the Pulleys left Roanoke Rapids he drove almost to Burlington, through Littleton and Warrenton, then south through Louisburg and west through Milton, Creedmoor, the edge of Durham, passing the city's tobacco warehouses in the dark, until a heavy fog and the glare of headlights off the mist tired him. He turned off the highway to park in a rural churchyard no more than thirty minutes' drive from Burlington.

Odell and the three children were asleep by then. Albert Pulley dozed too, planning to rest an hour and then drive on.

What woke him and the family seconds later was the sound of an approaching car, a hiss and crackle as it rolled closer to them. There was a quick, bright flash of light, a spotlight none of the Pulleys could see past. The beam caught them sleeping. None of them, waking in a rush, could see who held the light. It was a nearly defenseless position to be caught in. The sound of a man's voice coming from behind the light, shouting to the Pulleys, startled them all.

The owner of the voice stepped into the spotlight at Albert Pulley's door. He wore a pistol, badge and uniform of a deputy sheriff. Albert Pulley talked. He and the family were just moving to Burlington, had stopped just to rest, would move on again, if it was all right, at first light, he said. The deputy was satisfied.

An hour later, at dawn, the Pulleys left the churchyard and drove the rest of the way to their new home in Burlington, five rooms in an old apartment building. There was a small kitchen, a small bathroom, a small living room, and two bedrooms, one for Albert and Odell Pulley, the other for Bobby, Geraldine and Crystal Lee.

The first day of school in Burlington, Albert Pulley took his children to class himself. It was part of his way of setting out the new life. He alone had found the new job, then the new apartment. He alone enrolled Geraldine in grade school, and took Bobby and Crystal Lee to their new school, Walter Williams High, where Crystal Lee entered the ninth grade, and her brother the tenth. It was the biggest school building, with the most students, they had ever seen. Crystal Lee was enrolled in eight courses: algebra, English, general science, social studies, Bible, home economics, typing and shorthand. After school that first day, and on many days during that year, when Albert Pulley came home from the first shift at Haw River Mills, he and Crystal Lee slipped away from the small apartment to go riding in his car until suppertime.

But as close as the two were, there were strains between them, and trouble. The first of that was over Gilbert Newsome, Crystal Lee's boy friend. Back in Roanoke Rapids, Gilbert, Crystal Lee, her sister Syretha and Syretha's boy friend Walter had often met at the rollerskating rink. The boys would walk the girls home only if they knew Albert Pulley was away at the mill. Gilbert and Crystal Lee continued to correspond while Gilbert was in the Army, but Albert Pulley began intercepting his daughter's mail—opening Gilbert's letters, reading them, then handing them to Crystal Lee. Finally, he forbade her to write Gilbert at all. Crystal Lee had mailed the young soldier snapshots of herself, pictures of a voluptuous woman in tight skirt and sweater, with a composed, nearly sultry face. It took seeing her in bobby socks and loafers at times to remind Albert Pulley that his daughter was only a teen-ager, and imagining what Gilbert Newsome would think about those pictures was too much for Albert Pulley.

Perhaps Gilbert Newsome was not that important to Crystal Lee, and perhaps the young soldier was unable to compete with Albert Pulley. However it was, not even Albert Pulley's ultimatum, much less his censoring of Crystal Lee's mail, was enough to estrange father and daughter. A few weeks later a steam boiler blew at Haw River Mills, and Albert Pulley came home early from work. "Get your rags together," he told Crystal Lee. The two of them left Bobby, Geraldine and Odell Pulley a note on the kitchen table: Gone to the beach, be back tomorrow. Albert Pulley had traded in the Dodge on a 1948 Cadillac, an eight-year-old cruising car he had tuned to perfection. That night he and Crystal Lee drove to Virginia Beach, 250 miles. He bought her dinner, told her jokes, and surprised her with a cheap ring, one she has kept to this day. They slept in the Cadillac, parked by the beach, and walked on the sand in the morning.

Albert Pulley's spontaneity enveloped Crystal Lee. The following winter Crystal Lee was in tenth grade and worked afternoons at a florist's in downtown Burlington. There was a heavy snow one day, and when Crystal Lee came home from school to change clothes for work, there was her father. He had given some excuse at the mill so he could go home—to play in the snow. He wanted Crystal Lee to do the same. "I wanted to go to work that day because I needed the money, and I was scared I'd lose my job. But Daddy, he was just so disappointed because I had to go to work that I didn't go to work that day. And the next day the snow was still on the ground, and he didn't want to go to work. I let him go on and take me to work. The more I stayed there and thought about how upset Daddy was, well, I walked all the way home so that we could play in the snow," Crystal Lee says.

Pleasing her father took Crystal Lee's money as well. Her job at Moultrie's Florist was considered by her high school teachers to be part of her education, like home economics courses. The job gave her course credit toward a high school diploma, and the school released her for work (as it released hundreds of other children) shortly after noon. She worked until five-thirty every afternoon, Monday through Friday, for fifty cents an hour. She kept her wages, as well as the dollar and twenty-five cents a week lunch money her parents gave her, until she had saved fifty or seventy-five dollars. Often she made a present of these earnings, handing the money to Albert Pulley and saying it should be used for one family bill or another. The Pulleys paid a pharmacist's bill of more than one hundred dollars in that manner. But more often, Crystal Lee spent her savings directly on her father.

As long as he lived in Burlington, Albert Pulley was homesick for Roanoke Rapids. He never admitted this, but the family sensed it. In Roanoke Rapids, where his brothers and sisters still lived, he had always gone fishing or hunting at least once every week. In Burlington, he never did.

Even the soil around Burlington was different from that in Roanoke Rapids. Here it was red dirt, almost clay, an unnatural, rusting soil, hard as rock after a rain, and it smelled flat and metallic, not like the darker soil of his home, whose scent was musty and loamy. This red clay was everywhere Albert Pulley went around Burlington—after textile mills, it was the most prominent feature of the southern piedmont, that crescent of eroded hills, dusty pinewoods and small industrial cities that curves southwest from Burlington through Charlotte, North Carolina, Greenville, South Carolina, and on past Atlanta nearly to Birmingham, Alabama. And Albert Pulley hated it.

Crystal Lee saw the homesickness in her father, and every month or two she pulled her savings out of her dresser drawer and gave them to him to buy gas for a visit back home. She did not always do it soon enough.

On a Sunday in fall the year Crystal Lee was in the eleventh grade, Albert Pulley got drunk. Odell Pulley, who had been increasingly sickly since the move to

Burlington two years before, was resting on the living-room couch that afternoon. Crystal Lee was listening to records in the children's bedroom. And Albert Pulley was in the kitchen, drinking. The sale of any drink more alcoholic than beer or wine was illegal in Burlington then, but there was corn whiskey from bootleggers, and he had a half-gallon jug of it. He sat at the kitchen table and poured the liquor into a water glass, then chased it with a soft drink. It was his custom to keep drinking that way until either he or the corn whiskey was exhausted. He drank alone, in silence.

Crystal Lee had a new boy friend that year, Buddy Arnett, and the day before he had given her a ring. This might have meant an engagement to be married. Crystal Lee was not certain then, in the eleventh grade, that she wanted to marry anyone. But she was clearly of marrying age—her sister, Syretha, had married in the tenth grade, and her brother, Bobby, had dropped out of high school the summer before to marry a Burlington girl who lied about her age to get the license.

Crystal Lee went into the living room to show the ring to her mother. Odell Pulley had a box of family snapshots on her lap then, and she barely lifted her head from the pictures to nod at Crystal Lee's new ring and smile at her daughter. Crystal Lee walked into the kitchen next. By now, Albert Pulley was well into his jug. She walked behind him, turned, and put her hand in front of him at the table. He saw the ring at once. As far as Albert Pulley was concerned, engagement rings meant impending marriage. He did not object to Syretha's, nor to Bobby's, but to Crystal Lee's he did. He grabbed at her wrist, but Crystal snatched back her hand. He shouted at her, and that brought Odell into the kitchen, still holding the box of snapshots she had been looking at.

No one remembers what she said to Albert Pulley then. "I would beg Momma not to fuss with Daddy, especially when he was drinking. I mean, I never remember my daddy hitting my mother, but he would get in the car and he'd drive off real fast, and I was always scared he'd kill himself," Crystal Lee says. Now Albert Pulley's rage rose with each word. Crystal Lee stood in silence by the kitchen table. Suddenly he reached across the table. He grabbed the box of snapshots, took it out of his wife's hands, and shouted he would destroy every picture. His wife and daughter broke into sobs. Albert Pulley slammed the box on the tabletop. He stumbled drunkenly through the living room, looking for the car keys. While he was in the bedroom searching for the keys, Crystal Lee took the lid off the picture box. There were snapshots of Odell Pulley, of the Pulley relatives, of Syretha, Bobby, Geraldine and Crystal Lee, as babies and as young children, and pictures of Albert and Odell Pulley from their wedding. Crystal Lee grabbed what she could. All she managed to get, and hide in her hand behind her back, were some of the baby pictures. Then Albert Pulley walked heavily through the kitchen. He swept up the box without speaking. Odell and Crystal Lee heard his car speed away. None of the Pulleys ever saw those pictures again.

"From the ninth through the twelfth grade, all I could remember was my father drinking daily. I was a daddy's girl, and I had to be his leader. Momma, she couldn't do anything with him when he'd get to drinking. Daddy, he loved children, and they loved him. Maybe he got the satisfaction of being with children because they always looked up to him. Momma was always downing him for his drinking. And he was, really, he was an intelligent person. He could do about anything he wanted to do. I know Daddy used to get after Momma about fixing up. Like when she'd get up or something, she'd maybe wear the same pair of slacks. And Daddy always wanted her to fix herself up, because she was pretty. And I guess maybe Daddy just wanted a wife that, you know, he could be proud of. This is the way Daddy was," Crystal Lee says.

The year Crystal Lee was in the eleventh grade also was the year she went to work in the cotton mills. Even with Odell and Albert Pulley working, and Crystal Lee working part-time for the florist, there was not enough money. So, at the age of seventeen, like her parents, grandparents, uncles and aunts before her, Crystal Lee went to work in the mill. She did not want to do it. She had been thinking about going to beautician school in Raleigh, and suggested that now to her father. Albert Pulley said he had no money to send her to another town to live. Then Crystal Lee suggested she join the Women's Army Corps. "Nothing but whores join the WACs," Odell Pulley said. She found the mill job for her daughter. It was on the second shift, 4 p.m. to midnight, at Haw River, where Odell and Albert worked.

Odell Pulley was on third shift then, midnight to morning. She got home just in time to see Crystal Lee and Geraldine off to school. When Crystal Lee got home from school in the afternoon, she had just enough time to change to work clothes and leave. The mill was an old brick plant on a hillside overlooking the Haw River. It was in a mill village of the same name that bordered Burlington, and it was a dirty, gray place. An older woman met Crystal Lee on the floor of the weave room that afternoon. She was to teach Crystal Lee how to be a weaver. "I just couldn't see myself doing that for the rest of my life, knowing that Momma had been doing it ever since I could remember. I said ain't no way I'm about to stand at a loom and pull those ends through there." Two weeks later she asked for and got a job as a battery filler, feeding wooden shuttles wrapped with yarn into metal boxes on the sides of looms, spare shuttles weavers use to keep the threads going.

That first night Crystal Lee ate supper in a bathroom off the weave-room floor. The mill hands ate either on the work floor or in the bathroom, because no lunchroom was provided by the company. While she was eating her sack dinner, Crystal Lee noticed another woman. She was the mother of a boy she knew at high school, and Crystal Lee walked over to the woman to say hello. "When she found out that I went to school with her son, she asked me to please not say anything that she worked at the mill. She didn't want any of her son's friends to know it. I told her I wouldn't say anything. But I told her I wasn't ashamed of my parents being cotton-mill workers," Crystal Lee says.

By her eighteenth year, the events of Crystal Lee's life had taken on a pattern, neither unbearably confining nor particularly sustaining. She had seen it countless times in the lives of her parents, their friends, and her own friends. The mills were the center of this pattern, and because that was so common the mills themselves were not (although some particular mill jobs definitely were) viewed as a burden to be borne, nor as a source of comfort. They simply were there. By now, Crystal Lee had worked the second shift at Haw River Mills for nearly eighteen months. She got up for school at seven in the morning, came home to change clothes for work in the afternoon, came home from work after midnight, and went to sleep to ready herself for another day like the last one. The physical and mental demands of this routine slowed her schoolwork, and she had to attend summer school to graduate that year, as did many of her classmates who worked in the cotton mills.

That June, Crystal Lee and her friends began spending hot middays at a swimming pool, Lloyd's, west of Burlington on the road to Greensboro. One of her friends, whose name was Donna—she was in summer school with Crystal Lee—had a brother, Guy, just home from a hitch in the Marines and temporarily separated from his wife. One afternoon Donna had a date with Guy's best friend, Junior Wood, who had been in the Marines with Guy, and the three of them met Crystal Lee at the swimming pool. The two young men were a striking pair, both more than six feet tall, both hard-muscled from their Marine tours. Junior had blond hair and blue eyes and teased and joked with everyone he met. Guy was his opposite, dark-haired, brown-eyed and quiet. Donna hoped Crystal Lee and Guy would become a pair. But both young men, from the moment they met Crystal Lee, were after her instead.

There had been little trace of teen-ager's looks in Crystal Lee since her junior year in high school. Her figure was full, and seemed still lusher because she was short. In the past two years she had spent as much time in the company of older men, fellow mill workers, as with boys her own age, and she had learned how she affected them. Years later, looking back on that summer, Crystal Lee said, "Guy, he always tried to get in my britches, and I never would let him 'cause I knew if he ever did, well, he probably wouldn't ever see me no more anyway. So I just told Guy no, there ain't no way. You aren't divorced, and there probably wouldn't be any future in it for me. That's when I accepted a date with Junior, and Junior and I started dating. Typical man, he tried the same crap, and he found out he'd have to marry me before he'd get it."

That first afternoon at Lloyd's swimming pool, Junior Wood made known his intentions in traditional swimming-pool fashion. Crystal Lee was swimming by herself when two strong hands took her by the ankles and swiftly pulled her underwater. There was a kiss, and the two came to the surface. "You shouldn't have done that," Crystal Lee told Junior. "Well, I just wanted to kiss you," he said. That night Junior phoned Crystal Lee to ask for a date. She turned him down then, but by the end of June the two were dating steadily. By the end of July they wanted to marry each other, but there were two problems.

First, Junior wanted to go to college. The idea of Crystal Lee's going to college had not occurred to anyone, certainly not to Crystal Lee. She supported Junior in his hopes to go. Junior's parents were mill hands, and if he went to college—he wanted to go to the University of North Carolina in Chapel Hill—he would have to find the money himself. He hoped to win a football scholarship. It had been three years since he had played regularly, but he thought he had been a good enough high school halfback to play in college. He had kept in shape in the Marines. That summer he was a general laborer on construction projects around Burlington, and that too helped him keep fit. In July, Junior began driving to Chapel Hill for football tryouts.

"The deal was, if he got the scholarship, we wouldn't get married. Which was understandable," Crystal Lee says. "If he had a chance to go to college, he was going to take it. But he didn't get the scholarship." When that fell through, Junior applied for work at Western Electric's equipment plant in Burlington. But he had taken few mathematics courses in high school, and Western Electric turned him down because of that. They told him to try night school and come back later.

The second problem was Albert Pulley. Crystal Lee hoped her mother could help overcome his certain opposition, but she had to approach Odell Pulley with caution. She did not want to upset her mother, particularly now, because the illnesses Odell Pulley had suffered since her first year in Burlington were especially severe that summer. She missed work much of June and July, and had coughing and choking spells that lasted for days. In mid-July, Albert Pulley's sister-in-law persuaded Odell to admit herself to Duke Hospital in Durham, thirty miles from Burlington. She found she had thyroid troubles that the physicians said would force her to keep to a strict diet and require medication for the rest of her life. When Crystal Lee went to her mother for help, Odell was resting on the living-room couch.

"I went in and asked Momma what did the doctor say. And he had released her. She told me he had released her. So I said, 'Well, since you're all right, Junior and I are going to get married.' "

"Lord have mercy. I don't know what your daddy's going to say," Odell Pulley told her daughter. They spent the rest of the day in silence, waiting for Albert Pulley to wake up. He was working second shift at Haw River, and usually was up by one in the afternoon. When he awoke, Crystal Lee and Odell avoided him until he had bathed, eaten, and taken a seat on the living-room couch. "I walked over and sat down in his lap, and I told him that Junior and I were going to get married. And I remember crying then. I guess maybe I was crying because I knew he would be upset. And he said, 'Well, if that's what you want, then it is all right with me,'" Crystal Lee says.

On August 8, 1959, before a justice of the peace in Graham, another of the mill hamlets on the edges of Burlington, Crystal Lee Pulley and Omar Carlos Wood, Jr., were married.

No friends or neighbors, not Crystal Lee's nor Junior's, not the Pulleys' nor the Woods', and none of the friends and relations from Roanoke Rapids came to the wedding. None were invited. There was no reception after. This was not because the Pulleys had no money for it. Albert Pulley could always, in combination with relatives, produce a feast of sweet cakes and pies, platters of fried chicken, washtubs of boiled ham, dishes brimful of field peas, golden yams, fried okra, all that and homemade ice cream, and whiskey for the men and iced tea for the women and children. But he was not asked to do so, and no invitations were sent, no reception arranged, because Crystal Lee was afraid. She was desperately worried the night before, and all through her wedding day. Albert Pulley had said nothing, done nothing, not mentioned the marriage, since the day she had sat in his lap and told him of her hopes. But Crystal Lee was sure he would deal with her marriage in some terrible manner. The best she could expect, she thought, was a roaring-drunk father at her wedding.

On the wedding day, only Albert Pulley brought a guest. The guest was one of his friends from the mill, J. B. Younce. He helped Albert Pulley tie tin cans to the bumper of Junior's 1953 Chevrolet coupe, then Albert and J. B. went inside the red brick building the justice of the peace shared with an optometrist. When the newlyweds left, and had driven no more than a few blocks, Junior Wood stopped the car and untied the tin cans. That was all there was to that. From the time she awoke that day, to the time she left the justice of the peace's office a married woman, Crystal Lee did not see her father take a drink. She never knew during what was to come that night whether or not her father was drunk.

Two weeks before the wedding, Crystal Lee and Junior had found an apartment and paid the deposit. Their clothes, some furniture, a temporary supply of groceries, and a madeup bed waited for them. They had not mentioned a honeymoon, and neither did they tell anyone they would spend their wedding night in the apartment. Albert Pulley asked Crystal Lee what her plans for the night were, but she avoided the question and told him nothing. Junior and Crystal Lee drove directly from the wedding to their apartment. Junior left his coupe parked in front of the building. It is not clear whether Albert Pulley had been told casually some days earlier, in a slip of tongue perhaps, where the couple would make their new home. He may have followed them from the wedding. But all that afternoon and night, it seemed to be once every hour, Crystal Lee and Junior would hear a long shout of a car horn. Looking out the front window, they would see Albert Pulley driving slowly by in his old Cadillac. He would not wave, and they could not see his face clearly. They could see the car, and hear the horn, and nothing else.

For the first hours of the evening, Junior Wood took that regularly circling car as a wedding prank. Crystal

Lee was not so sure. They did not know that when he was not passing by the apartment, leaning on the horn longer and longer each time, Albert Pulley was at home. Odell begged him, in between trips, to stop it, to let this one be the last one, to leave them alone. He did not listen to her. On and on into the night, Albert Pulley drove by the apartment, once an hour. He did not stop by bedtime, he did not stop by midnight. Inside, Crystal Lee lay fully awake, watching the hands of the clock turn, tensing and tightening as the time came closer to the hour, not hearing the horn yet and imagining that this time he had stopped the car out front and would be at the door any moment; and then, finally, the horn would sound, going by in a tone first distant, then loud, then distant like the passing of a freight train, and Crystal Lee would begin another hour's wait.

Had Albert Pulley come into their apartment that night, roaring with drunkenness and anger, had he fought with Junior Wood, even struck down his daughter, it would have been less of a torture. There was only the relentless passing car and horn. By morning, Crystal Lee had not slept. She faced her first full day of marriage shrunken by the fears and imaginings of that night. Junior, not knowing Albert Pulley well, slept through the night. In the morning, shortly after Junior awoke and joined his bride, Albert Pulley knocked at the door, a wide grin on his face, with a hearty handshake for Junior. He had just dropped by for a cup of coffee.

Crystal Lee Wood was proud of her husband. Junior did not pity himself when the football coaches turned him down for a scholarship and ended his hopes of going to college. And when Western Electric told him he did not know enough math, Junior Wood did what they said. He enrolled in night school math courses. He gave up his construction work, too. He had been happy with it, enjoying the outdoors and the companionship of the other men, but it was only rough work, gang labor, and did not seem serious enough for a married man. So he gave up that and found a job in the cotton mills with his wife.

Crystal Lee had a new job, too. A friend told her she could make more money in a job at Glen Raven Mills, in another mill village on the west side of Burlington. She quit Haw River Mills, where Odell and Albert Pulley still worked, and took the new job. It was a curious one for her to hold. She was what is called a stop-checker. Her job was to stand behind the weavers' backs, timing them to see how fast they might rethread a loom, unstop a spindle, or complete a run of towels. She used a stopwatch and marked the results on a clipboard. A stop-checker is clearly a tool of mill management, enabling the bosses to see which weavers work well enough to hold their jobs, so stop-checkers are mistrusted and resented by other mill hands, and management has to offer more money to get mill hands to take the job. Crystal Lee often felt uncomfortable as a stop-checker. Years later she explained why. "When my parents worked in the cotton mill, there were a lot more people working in the textile part of it. I mean, like maybe there were fifteen to twenty weavers; where you go in the same mill today, it's only three or four weavers. This was caused by stop-checkers, where they'd put a stop-checker on a weaver and time them. If you could do this many, they'd give you that many more looms to do," she said. Weavers who once thought they could operate only two looms at a time learned they could operate four at a time—or they could find another job.

Junior worked at Glen Raven, too. He was an apprentice mechanic in the maintenance department, learning how to repair looms, the work Albert Pulley had been doing almost twenty years. Junior joined the company softball team, and Crystal Lee sat in the bleachers at the company ballpark and watched him play. He was a pitcher, and a good one. In Swepsonville, a mill town ten miles southeast of Burlington where Junior Wood lived as a child, he had led the Little League team to the state championship.

That first year of their marriage, Crystal Lee and Junior Wood were happy. They swam and picnicked in the summer and early fall. Junior helped with the housework. On Saturday nights they joined other couples from the mill to go out for dinner and dancing, sometimes in Greensboro, sometimes in Chapel Hill.

"Junior was a happy man. He laughed a lot, always cutting up a bunch of foolishness with people. But he was quick-tempered. He didn't take anything off anybody. He'd just as soon slap you as look at you if he didn't like what you said," Crystal Lee says, describing a man not unlike her father, and in many ways not unlike herself. That winter Junior and Crystal Lee drove often to Swepsonville to watch his sister play basketball on the Alexander Wilson High School girls' team. And in January, Crystal Lee became pregnant. "He was real excited when I got pregnant, and he was hoping it was a boy," Crystal Lee says.

Junior got his wish—the child, a boy, was born on October 20, 1960. "Junior didn't stay at the hospital with me when I was in labor. I sent him home because he was so upset. I told him to go on and go to work, because it wasn't any telling how long it would be before the baby was born. The nurses called him afterwards. I remember the first time he saw him. He couldn't get over how small he was. He brought a flower up there that had a little pair of boxing gloves on it. And he picked out Mark's name. I wanted to name him Dennis Jay after 'Dennis the Menace" on TV. But Junior named him Robert Mark. Robert was after a good friend of his, and Mark was after my granddaddy. He would help me take care of Mark; he would change his diapers and like that. He wasn't the type of man that was afraid he'd break if he held him," Crystal Lee said.

Albert Pulley was excited about the baby too. He came to visit often that fall, and he played with Mark and remarked on one or another Pulley quality he said he could see in his grandson, and it seemed that the way he said it always led to trouble.

Albert Pulley was no more reconciled to the marriage of Crystal Lee now than he was the night he circled the newlyweds' apartment and terrified his daughter. Junior Wood saw Pulley's stubbornness, and a contest soon grew up between the men. "Daddy and Junior used to get in a lot of scuffles," Crystal Lee says. "They'd get in an argument and they'd always fall into fighting. They'd always end up shaking hands, though." These were not simply pushing matches, or chest-to-chest standoffs; they were actual fights, with blows exchanged in full force and blood drawn purposefully and in anger. "They never could agree on nothing, and neither one would give in, so they'd always end up fighting about it. They would be talking, and the next thing I knew they would be fighting. I never could figure it out. Daddy would drink some, and maybe Junior had a couple of beers, and

Junior was the kind, he was always right about everything. And if he was right, man, he wasn't going to say he was wrong. I remember the first fight they got into. It really upset me. I really cried about it. After that, I said to myself, hell, y'all go on and fight, and whoever kills the other, well that's the way it goes."

It never came to that. Each man was strong enough and at times angry enough to kill the other, but they held their fights to bruises, bumps, blackened eyes and bloody noses. "Daddy never liked Junior, and the reason he never liked Junior was because he was a man. Like if Daddy would say something, most of the boys I ever went with, they'd always agree with Daddy no matter if he was wrong. But Junior wouldn't do that. And Daddy just felt, I'm sure, that Junior had taken his little girl away from him. I was always torn between Daddy and Junior because it was hard to hurt Daddy, and it was hard to hurt Junior. So that caused problems as far as my marriage went. It caused us to have problems. I was young, and I was jealous. Junior was young, and he was jealous," Crystal Lee says.

There was a married man in Burlington who had been a neighbor of the Pulleys when Crystal Lee was in high school. She used to go for rides with the man, and she let him know she liked him. There was no more to it than that, as far as Crystal Lee cared, but the man saw it differently. He even talked with Albert Pulley, saying he wanted to leave his wife and marry Crystal Lee. Albert Pulley whipped Crystal Lee with his belt for that, and told her not to spend any more time with the man. "He wasn't a real handsome man, but he was a real man," Crystal Lee says. And one night a few months after Mark was born, this man followed Crystal Lee home from work. There was no trouble, and the man left quietly when Crystal Lee told him to, but rather than leaving it at that, she told Junior about it. Junior went right out that night, found the man at his home, and gave him a beating.

A few weeks later, just before Christmas of 1960, Junior told Crystal Lee one morning on his way out the door that he would be home late that night, around eleven o'clock, because a group of men from the mill were having dinner and drinks together. No women, just the men, he said. "I had cleaned house that day. He went to the supper. 'Course the wives, they couldn't go, which was always disturbing to me. And of course it was twelve or one or two in the morning when Junior did come in, and I was mad as hell, fussing, what a lot of wives do. I wouldn't do it now, but I was young," Crystal Lee says.

Junior was drunk when he came in the front door. Crystal Lee was waiting up for him, sitting fully dressed in a rocking chair in the living room of their small apartment. She began in a low voice, hoping not to wake Mark. Junior would have none of it, none of the questions, none of the demands for an accounting of his time, none of the ridicule of his drunkenness, not the tone of her voice nor the anger in her words. The argument grew louder, to shouts and then a scream when Junior slapped Crystal Lee. She slapped him back. He turned about and stepped into the bedroom.

When he appeared before her again, Junior held a pistol in his hand. He waved it at Crystal Lee, forcing her to tilt the rocker back and back. Then he lifted the pistol and slammed the barrel across her nose. The weapon discharged. The bullet went harmlessly off through the ceiling, but the force of the pistol broke Crystal Lee's nose. Junior stepped back in surprise. Crystal Lee got to her feet and pushed by him. She went to the kitchen, holding her bleeding nose, and stood over the sink, crying and shaking with anger.

Junior did not follow her. He went to the bedroom, past Mark's crib, and fell fully clothed on the bed. By the time Crystal Lee found him there, Junior was snoring loudly, passed out. She slipped the car keys out of his pants pocket, and then wrapped Mark in blankets, carried the baby quietly out the front door, and drove home to Albert and Odell Pulley.

That morning Albert Pulley took Crystal Lee to the hospital. She had the broken nose set and was put in a hospital bed to rest. In the afternoon, Junior came by. She refused to let him in her room. Three days later, when Crystal Lee was discharged from the hospital, she went to a lawyer and had legal separation papers drawn. By the end of that week she and Junior had divided the furnishings in their apartment, and Crystal Lee and Mark were living with the Pulleys.

The terms of the separation gave Junior the right to see Mark at the Pulley home, and near the end of January he began going to their house, but only when Albert Pulley was at work. These visits slowly began to bring Junior and Crystal Lee back together. They felt they loved each other, had always done so, despite the fight, but Crystal Lee had moved so swiftly to get legally separated that neither of them had had time to think calmly about it. By the middle of February the two had buried their anger, and one cold, wet afternoon Crystal Lee told Junior she was ready to live with him again.

Rain, snow and sleet had fallen alternately all morning, and was still coming down when Junior left the Pulley home late that afternoon. "I had put Mark to sleep, and Junior had walked in there, and he was looking at him," Crystal Lee remembers. "He was real proud of Mark. I had told him that I would tell Momma and Daddy the next day that I was going back to him. So when he started out the door, it was snowing, sleeting a little bit, and I remember telling him, 'Junior, let me give you some newspaper so you won't get wet.'" She stood in the doorway and watched Junior run to his car, the newspaper over his head, heading for Alamance County Technical Institute, where he was taking night classes in math, still hoping to find a job outside the mills. Junior had a 1957 Chevrolet then, a Christmas present he had bought for himself, and he laughed and waved through the window to Crystal Lee when he drove away.

Her parents worked on the third shift at the mill that night, midnight to morning. Geraldine, Crystal Lee's younger sister, who was in high school then, was home. Soon after Albert and Odell Pulley left for work, Crystal Lee went to the bedroom she shared with her baby, pulled the crib closer to her single bed, and went to sleep.

At two o'clock that morning the ringing phone woke her up. Crystal Lee tiptoed past Mark's crib and ran quietly down the hall to the living room to answer the phone. "Lee, I'm at the hospital," the voice on the phone said. Crystal Lee recognized the voice—Sylvia, Junior's sister. "I'm up here at the hospital, and Junior's been killed," Sylvia said.

"I just didn't believe it," says Crystal Lee. "I said, 'What in the world are you talking about? What are you trying to do?' and I just hung up the phone. I just started crying, and Geraldine came in there and I told her. I said somebody just called here and told me that Junior is dead. I said I don't believe it. So I got the phone book and looked up Alamance County Hospital, and I called out there to the emergency room, and I told the lady, I said, 'Look, I just got a phone call from someone claiming to be my husband's sister —Omar Carlos Wood, Jr.—and says that he's been in an accident, and he's dead.' And she said, 'That's right.' That's the way I found out that Junior was dead."

Geraldine took the phone from her sister and called Haw River Mills: Albert and Odell Pulley came home in minutes.

Junior Wood had gone to night school, then met a friend who teased him into racing his 1957 Chevrolet. The two friends had several beers, and went off to drag race. Out on the Swepsonville Road, in front of Alexander Wilson High School, on the road Junior and Crystal Lee used to take to go see his sister play basketball, Junior Wood raced his car. In the snow and the sleet and the darkness, Junior pulled up to his friend's car, and was trying to pass when he lost control. He died a few blocks from home.

"I remember going to the funeral home. This man comes to the door. I wanted to go in and see Junior, but he said he didn't have him prepared, and he didn't think it would be a good idea for me to see him. I really wanted to see him, but Daddy wouldn't let me go in. It was snow on the ground, and Daddy and Mommy took me down to Mr. and Mrs. Wood, and they were very kind. They let me make the arrangements. A lot of his friends came by. And that was the end of Junior, as far as that goes," Crystal Lee says.

Crystal Lee entered a time when her life was filled by an emptiness. As the days passed it spread all about her. Her routines became dulled because no small pleasures were left untouched by the void, and the loss of those small pleasures became themselves a steady reminder of the emptiness. Some women try to fill this void with men, and this works as long as the woman is both clever enough to disguise her purpose and lucky enough to avoid men who can detect and deny the slight hungry air about her. Other women, or men, allow a certain numbness to dull the emotion brought on by emptiness, but a numbed body cannot feel injury even though that injury is still real and damaging.

In the months following Junior Wood's death, Crystal Lee lived on at the Pulleys' house with her baby. "Now I know that at that time I was under a great deal of pressure. I now know why Momma and Daddy would watch me so close. They didn't want me to go off by myself. I think maybe they thought I might not keep my mind on where I was going or whatever," Crystal Lee says. She did not go back to work in the mills. She filled the space of her days caring for Mark and keeping house for her parents.

One day, when Odell Pulley was home from work, Crystal Lee and her mother went out on some errands. One errand took the two women to a small family store, the kind that is as much dime store as grocery. The store was owned and managed by the parents of Miles Simmons,* a boy whom Crystal Lee had dated in high school and who had taken her to the senior prom. He was now at the University of North Carolina in Chapel Hill. His mother was in the store that day, and she spoke to Odell and Crystal Lee. She had read about Junior's death in the newspaper, she said, and was sorry to hear of it. Her son's name came up in the conversation, and Crystal Lee, who had not seen

*Not the boy's real name.

him since marrying Junior, told the woman he should drop by to see her the next time he was home from college. The following Sunday he did.

There were Pulley relatives visiting from Roanoke Rapids that day. They were inside playing with Mark, so Crystal Lee and Miles Simmons sat in his car out front, talking about high school days and telling each other what had happened to them in the years since. Crystal Lee was twenty-one then, and Miles Simmons twenty-two. "He was always a woman's man, and I didn't want to be tied down by him. He had a roving eye, and I didn't want that for my man," Crystal Lee says. But Simmons was fun to be with, a good dancer, shorter and smaller than Junior Wood, but a slight, handsome boy with dark hair and dark eyes. Junior had been dead four months, and Miles Simmons was Crystal Lee's first date as a widow. It led to a short affair, in May of 1961.

The two made love twice, each time in the Pulley living room, late after midnight, while Crystal Lee's parents were on the third shift at the mill, and her sister Geraldine slept in the next room. "I remember the second time. I just told him right then, I said, 'You know what? I have a feeling that I'm pregnant.' It took so long for Junior and I. I wanted a baby so bad, and it seemed like it took forever for me to get pregnant with Mark. I just thought I couldn't have children. And there it was with him, the second time. So I wouldn't see him any more. He'd call, or he'd come over, and when I found out for sure that I was pregnant, I did go to him, and I called him and told him. He wanted to marry me. He even talked about quitting school, going into the Army so he'd have a job. And I told him that I knew that he was going to college, and that I didn't think it would be right for me to marry him, and he'd probably have to quit school. And he'd always resent that fact, that I was the cause of him having to quit school. I really didn't think that he was mature enough to be father to Mark. I was thinking more about the child that was living, more than the one I was carrying, but I realize now that I should have married him, just for the name, for the child's sake," Crystal Lee says.

Miles Simmons went back to college; Crystal Lee would not see him until ten months later. She and Albert Pulley began their afternoon rides again. They talked for hours as he drove around Burlington, but Crystal Lee did not mention her pregnancy. In June, two months pregnant, she returned to her job as stop-checker at Glen Raven Mills. One of the weavers she had to time, a man, began to taunt her. He ran, literally, from loom to loom when Crystal Lee appeared with her stopwatch and clipboard. She was unable to keep up with him. "I tried to tell him the faster you work, the more work they'll put on you," Crystal Lee says. But the man laughed at her and ran whenever she tried to time him. Finally she refused to check him at all. Her floor supervisor told her to, and when Crystal Lee told her story of the weaver's racing from loom to loom, the supervisor would not believe it. Crystal Lee refused to change her mind. She was taken to the office and fired.

Crystal Lee felt more abandoned than ever. She still told no one of her pregnancy. "I even thought about taking something, for an abortion, but I didn't know what in the world to take," she says. If she had not been entirely alone, fired from the mill, afraid to tell Albert Pulley about her pregnancy, unwilling to go to the father of the child she carried, who in any case might not have been much help—had she not been cut off from all these more normal sources of help, Crystal Lee almost certainly would not have gone to the county welfare office.

In mill-hand society, as among dirt farmers, a man looks to his own, rarely asking for help, and that only from his family. Welfare is held to be demeaning, not just to social status, but to a man's self-respect as well. Welfare, Crystal Lee had always heard from Albert Pulley, is what blacks get, and if there is one thing a white mill hand knows, because he has been told it so often by his bossman, his politicians and his preacher, it is this: whatever else a mill hand is, he is at least above a nigger.

White women from mill-hand towns are raised to believe this, but unlike their brothers, they are not taught, nor expected, to look to their own. A man will do that for them. In November of 1961, when she was seven months pregnant, Crystal Lee went alone to the Alamance County welfare office in Burlington. She was directed to a woman who wrote down her name and filled out some papers, then Crystal Lee was given a bottle of vitamin pills and the address of a physician in Mebane, a village ten miles east of Burlington. Just before Crystal Lee left the welfare office, the woman told her of a place in Durham for unwed mothers, and suggested Crystal Lee go there during her final months of pregnancy, have her illegitimate child there, and give up the baby for adoption.

"What I was trying to do was work it out to where people wouldn't know. I wanted to keep the baby, and I figured if I could get another start in another town, that I would be all right with the children. But I also knew that Daddy would never go along with that; he just wouldn't understand," Crystal Lee says. She considered giving up the baby for adoption, and almost at once rejected it. "I could never live with myself, saying, 'Where is it? Who's got it?' " she said.

She went out to the cemetery west of Burlington every day for a week after that trip to the welfare office. Crystal Lee sat on the ground next to Junior's grave and tried to decide what to do. Although she was seven months pregnant, no one asked her about it. Instead, she was kidded about putting on weight. She knew that would not go on much longer. A few days after Thanksgiving, Crystal Lee bundled up Mark, put him in the car, and drove to Durham. She found the address given her by the woman in the welfare office. It was a large white clapboard antebellum house, two stories, with attic windows above that, set back from the street in an old neighborhood of the city. For an hour, Crystal Lee and Mark sat in the car in front of the big house. "I didn't even go up to the door. I just sat in the car, and sit there and sit there. And then I just drove on back to Burlington. I never went back over to the welfare department. I would think about it.

"Daddy and I kept on taking our rides, while Momma was cooking supper, and finally one day I broke down and I told Daddy that I was pregnant. He said, well, he sorta suspected it, you know. He asked me who it was, the father, and I told him, and he said, well. He wasn't as upset as I thought he was going to be, and actually I thought he was glad. I felt like he was glad because, well, there he had me again to where I'd have to stay at home and depend on him," Crystal Lee says.

One month and ten days after her twenty-second birthday, Crystal Lee gave birth to another boy. She named him Albert, after her father, and Jay, after J. B. Younce, her father's friend who had been at the wedding of Crystal Lee and Junior Wood.

Crystal Lee had no familiarity with the law, nor with lawyers, beyond the time she had legal separation papers drawn. Albert Pulley was equally lost when his daughter asked him what she should do to get support for Jay from the father. Crystal Lee sent Miles Simmons a certified letter in February, telling him she was at her parents' home with the new baby, and that he could come see his child if he wanted to, and that she wanted a meeting, to discuss money. "He came on by one day. He said he had no money, that he was in college. I told him I had enough problems without him adding to it, and however he wanted to support him was fine with me, but he was going to support his own child," Crystal Lee says. She told Simmons she had been to a lawyer, and that he could either make arrangements to help support Jay, or go to court in a paternity suit.

Simmons at first refused to admit he was father of the child. Crystal Lee's lawyer and his lawyer met, and the two men agreed to a settlement out of court. It was $4,000, half to be paid that year, half the next year, and in return Crystal Lee had to sign an agreement releasing Simmons from any further obligations. The papers were signed in a judge's chambers, with only the judge, her lawyer, Simmons' lawyer and Crystal Lee present. "It made me feel dirty, and he was just as guilty of it as I was, and yet I was the one having to face these men. And I didn't think it was right, but what could I do?" Crystal Lee says.

One day as she stood at the washing machine, folding diapers, it occurred to her to wonder how much longer she could live here, in her parents' home in Burlington. Junior Wood had died sixteen months before. Mark was two years old now, Jay six months old, and she, Crystal Lee said to herself, was twenty-two years old and "felt like I was going insane."

"It was the same old story with my daddy," Crystal Lee says. "He was always very possessive of me. He didn't want me to go anywhere unless he went. I wasn't dating then. I tried to before, but Momma, she wouldn't keep the kids for me to go out because it upset Daddy, and she didn't want him upset with her. I had to leave the children with baby-sitters, but it seemed like every time I did that, Daddy would get so upset it just wasn't worth it." Albert Pulley took Crystal Lee riding in the car with him almost every day, to the grocery, or downtown on a shopping errand, just as he had when she was a young girl. Crystal Lee was not working, and the rides with her father were almost the only times she left the house.

"I was dating this one guy, but that was on the sly. He was a truck driver, and I'd call to his office to see when he was due back in town. He had a cabin out on a lake, and we went there. I took the children with me every time. He wanted to marry me, but he drank too much. I didn't want Mark and Jay to have a daddy who drank too much," she said.

The only other times she left her parents' home, and Burlington, were occasional weekends to visit Walter and Syretha Medlin, her older sister and her brother-in-law, in Roanoke Rapids. During one of those weekends, when Crystal Lee and her sister were in the kitchen, Syretha told her to come to the window. Syretha pointed to a young man in the back yard of the house behind them. His name was Cookie Jordan, Syretha said, and he was single—or at least getting a divorce. His wife had run off with another man. Walter worked at the paper mill with Cookie—both drove forklift trucks—and in fact, before Junior Wood died, he, Cookie, and Walter had gone fishing together several times. As Syretha was telling Crystal Lee all this, Walter came into the kitchen and saw who they were looking at. He said to Crystal Lee, "I ought to introduce you to Cookie." Perhaps she saw no point then in meeting a man who lived so far from Burlington. All she said to Walter was, "Uh-huh."

But then, on a Sunday in the early summer, when Syretha and Walter were leaving Burlington after spending the weekend with the Pulleys, Walter turned to Crystal Lee and said, 'You ought to come see us sometime." She surprised Walter when she looked him straight in the eyes and quietly said, "You know, Walter, I just might do that one of these days. I just might pack up my things and come see you all."

She did not want to stay in Burlington any longer. Too many places there reminded her of Junior Wood, and too many times it seemed she had to overcome feeling guilty and look right back in the eyes of friends who knew she had given birth to an illegitimate child.

That week Crystal Lee finally told Albert Pulley she was moving. "It took me a long time to work up my courage. Daddy didn't say too much. I guess he could see I had my mind made up," Crystal Lee says. She moved on a Saturday late in June, leaving behind the few furnishings she and Junior had, a washing machine and a bedroom suite, dishes and kitchenware, for Albert Pulley to bring when she found work and a home of her own. This time Albert Pulley had nothing to say.

2

THE MILL HANDS in Roanoke Rapids think of their little town as ninety miles from everywhere: ninety to Raleigh, the North Carolina state capital; ninety to Richmond, over the line in Virginia, where the bankers and merchants who colonized the town came from; ninety miles to Norfolk, the place the mill hands think of when they say let's go to the city. This geographical remoteness and the insular character of the cotton mills themselves have produced a backwater town where change is slow and slight. That is the way the cotton-mill owners want it.

There was nothing there but virgin pine forest—no town, no settlement, not a country store nor a farmhouse—until 1895. That year a former Confederate Army officer, Major Thomas Leyburn Emry, built a small hydroelectric power plant on the Roanoke River. "The Cotton Mill Campaign" was in its final years in the Deep South then, and Southern politicians, merchants and bankers offered cheap power, cheap labor and cheap land to New England cotton-mill owners if they would move their plants south. Major Emry's power plant was part of that campaign, and his first customer was a wealthy Yankee, John Armstrong Chaloner, an heir to the Astor family fortune. Chaloner built a knitting mill on the Roanoke River next to the Major's power plant.

Chaloner hired fifty workers. Since the countryside was virgin forest right to the gates of his new mill, Chaloner also built thirty houses to rent to his mill hands. In 1897, Major Emry and investors from Richmond built a second mill, the Roanoke Mills Company, to make flannel and towels. The Major hired 225 mill hands, and as Chaloner had before, the Major built a village of houses to serve his mill. That year the North Carolina legislature incorporated the two mill villages into one town. Major Emry chose the name, Roanoke Rapids, and Major Emry was the first mayor. He owned the power company, his mill, his houses, all the land in the town, and all the forests around town. He built the first two streets, and the first two commercial buildings on them. He opened the only saloon, and he donated the land for the town's only church.

When he formed his mill, Major Emry hired a native North Carolinian, Sam F. Patterson, to run it. Patterson was a bull-voiced man, big and rough, shrewd and ambitious. Three years after he arrived, Patterson and another group of Richmond investors formed a third mill, the Rosemary Manufacturing Company, to make woven table damask. Patterson bought land from the Major, one mile south of the Major's mill. He hired a hundred hands and built more rows of tenant houses. Patterson's brother, John, moved to town and founded a bank, which got the accounts of his brother's and the Major's mills. Chaloner's mill, the first in town, went bankrupt in 1900. But the other mills prospered. Interlocked as they were, with Major Emry owning the power plant, most of the land, much of the bank, and his own mill, Emry and Patterson owned the town, from the ground to the top brick of the mills, all its streets, all its houses, all its stores. And they provided every job there was.

Patterson and Emry built nearly eight hundred tenant houses in Roanoke Rapids before 1918. Each house had electricity, because the Major's power plant sold it. But there was no sewer system and no water system. The mill hands carried water by hand from wells dug throughout the two villages. In summer, malaria and typhoid infested the wells, and mosquitoes and flies infested the back-yard privies. Roanoke Rapids was a death trap in hot weather, and quinine and calomel were the only defenses the workers had against shaking ague and malarial inertia. Still, the mills never had trouble finding enough workers, young men and women, whole families, giving up farming to move to the mill villages. An entire family rarely earned more than ten dollars a week, and that they rarely saw, after deductions for rent, electricity, clothes and food at the company stores.

Sam Patterson built a third mill in 1910. He named it after himself and brought 275 more mill hands to town to make ginghams, chambrays and flannels. He built a fourth mill, Roanoke #2, in 1917, to make automobile-tire yarn, and by 1919 he had enough money to buy out the Richmond bankers and persuade Major Emry to sell him his mills as well.

Sam Patterson was more than merely the principal

employer in Roanoke Rapids. By himself and through his mill bosses, Patterson also was the town's landlord, its merchant, its mayor, school principal, police chief, and patron of social and religious welfare. It was not until 1913 that the first privately owned house was built in Roanoke Rapids, just outside the town limits, where it remains today. The large homes for Patterson and his senior supervisors were built on mill lots, and Sam Patterson retained title. His mills built, staffed and paid for the only public schools in town. His mill hands staffed the volunteer fire department, using equipment he bought. He supplied the instruments and hired the instructor for the town's brass band, and every summer he chartered a train, shut down the mills for a day, and sent all his workers to the beach. His store supplied seed and tools, and he set aside plots of land for the mill hands to turn into vegetable gardens. He hired home economists to supervise the mill women in community cannery kitchens that he had built.

And if such a life was too hard for a mill family, man, woman or child—for all worked in the mills—no one complained for long. Except for a few workers at a small paper mill on the riverbank (even its products were sold to Patterson's mills) and a handful of merchants whose well-being depended on Sam Patterson's tolerance, everyone in Roanoke Rapids worked at the cotton mills, lived in the mills' houses, shopped at the mills' stores, sent their children to the mills' schools, and ate out of the mills' gardens. If a mill hand gave up his job, he and his family gave up all the rest as well. And since there was nothing else in Roanoke Rapids, that meant getting out of town.

No feudal baron controlled and shaped the lives of his serfs as much as Sam Patterson molded those of his mill hands for more than a quarter-century in Roanoke Rapids. The pattern of one-man control Sam Patterson established in Roanoke Rapids continued after his death in 1926 through his own right-hand man, Frank Williams. He ran the town the way Patterson had run it, first for the Simmons Mattress Company, which bought all six of Patterson's mills in 1928, and then for J. P. Stevens & Company, Inc., which bought the six mills from Simmons in 1956. The men who ran the mills controlled the town, and made Roanoke Rapids the shut-off, contained society it is today.

There is a continuity in all this control, and the mill hands in Roanoke Rapids today are aware of it. The company reminds them of it on bulletin boards, and at occasions such as Fourth of July picnics. The daily newspaper in Roanoke Rapids reminds them of it every year in a special edition celebrating the mills. But the mill hands have a closer, more personal knowledge of the ways their lives are tied to the mills. Most of the workers today are second- and third-generation mill hands whose parents remember Frank Williams, and whose grandparents remember Sam Patterson. Every day they go to work, they go to the same six brick cotton mills, the same buildings where their parents and grandparents worked, where the only difference now is that the mill is bigger.

The old Roanoke mill Major Emry built still produces towels, only it has five hundred workers now. The old Patterson mill still produces towels, with six hundred workers now. Sam Patterson's old Rosemary mill still produces damask, but now with a thousand mill hands. His old bleach, dye and print mill now has three hundred workers, bleaching, dyeing and printing cloth. Patterson's Roanoke #2 has 250 mill hands making polyester cotton sheeting now instead of automobile-tire yarn. Albert and Odell Pulley worked in that mill, the same building, on the same plank wood floors, at the same Jacquard looms, literally the same machines, that Sam Patterson perfected, patented and installed in 1919. When their daughter Crystal Lee moved back to Roanoke Rapids, she eventually went to work in the sixth of the old mills, now called the Roanoke Fabricating Plant. And one of the people she met in Roanoke Rapids was the son of another mill family, the Jordans, who worked the same cotton mills and lived, for a short time, in the same rows of mill houses.

In early July 1936, the middle of the American Depression, there were nine persons living under the tin roof of a shotgun house, the last house on the river end of Monroe Street in Roanoke Rapids. The house was in the Bunker Hill section, part of the first mill village built in town, and was rented from Simmons by Lucy and Larry Jordan. It had no indoor plumbing, it had a potbelly stove in the front room for heat, and it had five rooms: two upstairs and three downstairs. Lucy Jordan was a weaver in the cotton mills and her husband was a maintenance worker for Simmons. Both were the first in their families to work the mills. Their parents were farmers.

Lucy Jordan had borne six children—Estelle, Dorothy, Myrtle, Robert, Harvey and Tiny—and was pregnant with a seventh. Her uncle lived in the small house as well, and the birth of the seventh child that month—July—made ten residents in the house. The child was named Larry Jordan, Jr., and he was conceived, he has since learned, during one of his father's occasional spells of living at home. The father was a rambling man, given to long, unexplained absences from home, shying away from his growing family, dissatisfied with mill work. "He would come to see Momma, but he didn't come to stay," her son remembers.

Larry Jordan quit the mills a few months after the birth of his seventh child. He opened a soup and sandwich luncheonette for workers at the Patterson and Rosemary mills. The decision made him one of the few persons in town not working in the cotton mills, and it cost his family their house, because the mills would not rent to any family whose members left their employ, not even if one member of that family continued working in the mills, as Lucy Jordan did, and as her uncle did also.

There was hardly any place in town for the family to live other than a crumbling building at the opposite end of town, on Roanoke Avenue, the main street. It had a grocery downstairs and several small apartments upstairs. The building was twenty yards from the Seaboard railroad tracks, in a neighborhood of old wood and tin shacks where the poorest mill hands from Rosemary lived. Across the street was a cotton gin and a row of small shops, including a barbershop, patronized by the few blacks living in Roanoke Rapids. Larry Jordan's sandwich shop, where a forty-cent lunch might consist of a large bowl of navy beans, a hot dog, two slices of bread and a soft drink, was two blocks down the street and around the corner, on 13th Street. The entire neighborhood, from 13th Street south to the Seaboard tracks and on either side of Roanoke Avenue, was called "The Junction."

Just as Albert Pulley shaped Crystal Lee's views of men and marriage, so did Larry Jordan shape his youngest child's views of marriage and family, leaving the boy a picture of how it ought not to be. "I don't ever remember, I don't remember one time my daddy ever giving me a penny. I know he had a little bit, I mean he had a nickel or a dime once in a while. He could have give to the kids. But he never did. I always remember him sending me to the store after some pipe cleaners—he smoked a pipe, not a cigar, and he didn't mess with cigarettes. It seemed to me pipe cleaners were three cents for a pack of them things. And I'd try to hold back on them pennies, and every time he'd throw out that hand, say, 'Let me have it, boy.' I never made it with them pennies, not a time," his son, Larry Jordan, Jr., says. The son came to be known as "Cookie." No one in the family remembers how he got the nickname, but by the age of six it had stuck.

When Cookie Jordan was two years old, his family moved out of the apartment in "The Junction" and across the railroad tracks, two blocks south, to 105 Clinton Street. It was a house rented from a wealthy farmer who had built a dozen wood-frame houses in what had been a cotton field. The farmer's little subdivision was the first rental property in town the mills did not own. Cookie lived in that house for sixteen years, until he graduated from high school in 1954 and went away in the Air Force. His father, however, rarely was there. "Daddy was a woman's man. He just couldn't leave women alone. That's all there was to it. He just couldn't do it. He just wasn't going to be tied down," Cookie says. When Cookie was seven years old his father left home for good with another woman. He came back occasionally, and when he did, he stayed with Lucy. No one could say when those times would be, nor how long he would stay, but he was always, if not welcome, at least taken in by Lucy Jordan. And he was always a figure of mystery and remoteness to his youngest son, who looked forward to each visit, and who was always let down, in one way or another.

On one such visit, when Cookie was eight years old, his father took him shopping for a baseball glove. One thing led to another that afternoon, a greeting on the street to a beer with a friend, until finally the stores closed. Larry Jordan sent his son home alone with a promise to get the mitt some other time. "He never did, never did. The first baseball glove I had, I bought it from a boy. Gave him a quarter for it. And I earned that money shining shoes," Cookie says. His memories of his father are scarce, and many are vague. Cookie has no memories from childhood of the violent wars between the old textile unions and the cotton-mill owners, nor does he recall the union being mentioned at home. Lucy Jordan was not a member. But one of his memories of his father is of the time Larry Jordan came home on a visit, flushed with feistiness, cocky and proud, having just spent the night in jail in Tarboro, another North Carolina mill town sixty miles south, where he had been marching through the streets with the United Textile Workers union. In 1946, when he was ten years old, Cookie and one of his sisters went with their mother to the hospital in Rocky Mount. There in bed was his father, the first time Cookie had known him to be sick. That night, Larry Jordan, Sr., died of cancer.

His death did not alter the outward routine of Lucy Jordan's life. She kept weaving at the looms in Simmons' mill, in the Rosemary plant ten blocks from her home on Clinton Street, and she kept raising her seven children. Her youngest, Cookie, was closest to her, and the boy drew his images of the way women should be, especially the way a wife and mother should be, from her. He saw her come home at the end of the first shift in late afternoon, her hair coated with cotton lint she did not take time to comb out. As soon as she was home, Lucy Jordan put on supper, never much meat, mostly cornbread, potatoes, vegetables from her garden behind the house. And while that cooked, she worked the garden, or scrubbed clothes on a washboard in a big tin tub on the back porch. To this day Lucy Jordan is, to her son Cookie, the most remarkable and praiseworthy woman he has ever known.

Cookie Jordan's early childhood years were those of World War II, and the mills ran full shifts day and night to fill military orders for cloth of all kinds. Then, and during the years immediately after the war, the town of Roanoke Rapids was the town it had been in Sam Patterson's day. Baskets of fruit went to the mill hands at Christmas, a gift from Simmons. There was still the July day off for the chartered train ride to the beach. There were no automobiles in the neighborhood where Cookie lived, and the only paved road in town was Roanoke Avenue. The canneries still were in use—Lucy Jordan used the one at Rosemary—and the mills still owned the houses their workers lived in, and the hospital. There were a few changes. Plumbing was put in the tenant houses for the first time during the Depression, when the federal government sent scores of Works Progress Administration men to town to do the job. The "bean wagon" did not run any more—although this long, horse-drawn cart had moved through the rows of mill village houses for decades, until the late 1930s, its driver sounding a hunter's horn, and women had brought lunch pails out to the wagon to be taken to their husbands at the mills.

Cookie took lunch to his mother during the summers, and these errands gave him his first look at the inside of a cotton mill. He walked right to his mother's loom to hand her her lunch, but he never stayed long. The vibrations of the floor, shaken by the looms, and the noise of the looms, the heat, and the closeness, the flying lint, pushed in on him. "It felt like it was going to suck the breath out of me. I felt so relieved when I got outside and could get some air," Cookie says. Even at home, in bed at night, Cookie could hear and feel the looms.

There is no "extra" money at all in such a mill family's life, not even enough money for food, clothes and shelter, so each of Lucy Jordan's seven children went to work as soon as possible—in the cotton mills, of course, when they were of high school age (Cookie's three older sisters still work there)—and before that, at any job they could find. Cookie was a shoeshine boy at the age of seven, an accomplished hustler who started with one can of black polish, one rag, and a box built for him by the husband of one of his sisters. He had a partner, also seven, a boy named Joe Harris. They worked the bus station during World War II, shining boots and shoes for sailors, soldiers and marines passing through town, and sometimes they made three or four dollars a day. By the time he was eleven, Cookie and Joe Harris had staked out one end of Roanoke Avenue as theirs alone for the shoeshine trade. Joe Harris took one side and Cookie the other.

The two boys were close friends, but Cookie considered himself far luckier than Joe Harris. That boy's mother, who also worked in the cotton mills and who also had seven children to feed, possessed the strongest hand for beating a child that Cookie had ever seen, as well as the loudest voice he had ever heard call a child home. She made Joe Harris stay outside all day. "Cold, rain, it didn't matter to that woman. Joe had to stay out. Me, we never had much, but I could always go home, go inside, any time I wanted to," Cookie says.

When Cookie and Joe Harris were in school they were inseparable. And they often collected a gang of pals on Saturday afternoons and loafed around the black barbershop on Roanoke Avenue, where they could pick fights with black boys, "if there wasn't too many of them," Cookie remembers. They played sandlot baseball in a field near the Rosemary mill, and fished in a creek near Clinton Street. They hunted squirrels and rabbits in the woods that still grew to the edge of town.

All Lucy Jordan hoped, or expected, her children to get from going to school was to be slightly better off than she, that education would lead her children to a job better than hers. Only one of her seven children graduated from high school, and that was Cookie. "Momma, she didn't see the importance of it. I mean the real importance. She'd tell me, 'Son, you need to graduate from school. You need to do that.' But she thought doing that I could do just a little better than what she did, and anything was better than that," Cookie says. There was no encouragement, no discipline to get more out of the books and classes than what was necessary to graduate. Cookie Jordan often says that if he had only had more encouragement in school, perhaps things would be better for him now.

By 1950, when he was a freshman at Roanoke Rapids High School, Cookie had decided to become a professional baseball player. Even though he was only fourteen years old, his decision was not taken lightly, nor was it uncommon among boys his age in town. The mechanics of becoming a professional athlete were not at all mysterious to boys in Roanoke Rapids.

These were the glory years of minor-league baseball, and Roanoke Rapids had a major-league farm club in the old Coastal Plain League. Cookie went every time he could get ticket money. He played sandlot baseball in grade school, and Little League baseball as well. He was good enough, as a centerfielder, to make the town all-star team that advanced to the North Carolina finals one year, going all the way to the championship game and then losing to the Little League team from Swepsonville, the mill village Junior Wood was from. "I think about it, he may have been on that ball team," Cookie says.

The cotton mills had their teams too, semi-professionals hired by the mills to play ball and entertain the mill hands. Cookie played pickup ball against the mill teams at times, and he played baseball for the high school team. But his dream of playing professional baseball did not work out. "I really believe if I had of went to the right school, and the right coach had of put the right word in for me at the right time, I believe I could have made it, 'cause I was pretty good," Cookie says.

There is not that much for him to remember from his school days. "I remember I had to wear gallus overalls, with knee patches. They were neat, but still, it was a patch, and I had to wear them to school. I didn't notice anybody else doing that, and they did, I'm sure they did, but I just didn't notice anyone else doing that. I felt like I was the only one," he says. He remembers going to the clinic owned by the mills, and says of those visits: "We had to sit on benches and wait to get in. But the doctors' children, and the lawyers' and businessmen's, they went right in. I saw these things, and I felt they were wrong then, but that was the way we were treated."

One of Cookie's high school courses was in textiles

—not the theory, history or management of the industry, but how to work in the mills, how to be a weaver or loom fixer. Albert Pulley, Crystal Lee's father, taught this course one year, although Cookie does not remember him from those days. He does remember going to high school with Syretha, Crystal Lee's older sister, but not Crystal Lee. There was another girl in his life then, Eloise Hale, a short, slightly plump brunette, a pretty girl one class behind him in high school. Her parents worked in the mills too, and her brother and Cookie often camped and fished together. That was how they met. Cookie stayed with the Hales one night so he could get up early to fish with the brother. At the time he was taking medicine for headaches and had to be awakened during the night. Eloise Hale woke him that night, gave him the medicine, and they began dating that week. They dated each other through high school, until 1954 when Cookie graduated.

He joined the Air Force, a four-year enlistment, and went off to San Antonio, Texas, for basic training—his first long trip away from Roanoke Rapids. Eloise stayed behind to finish high school, and it was a matter of course to them that they married. Cookie was home on leave, in April of 1955. Eloise was working afternoons as a secretary for an ophthalmologist. It was a big wedding, for a mill hand's daughter, and they held it in the Rosemary Baptist Church. Two weeks later, Cookie was back on duty in El Paso, Texas, and waiting for him there were orders for overseas, to Japan.

When he thinks about it, about his life, it seems to Cookie Jordan that if so many things had happened, so many things that strike him as beyond his influence, never subject to his control, if some certain things along the way had gone differently, he might be happier today. If his father had stayed home and not rambled; if his mother had pushed him in school; if the baseball coach had put in the right word; if he had not been sent to the Far East so soon after marrying Eloise; and—most importantly, he sometimes says—if his brother Harvey had not died.

That was before Cookie joined the Air Force and got married. If Harvey had lived, Cookie says he might never have done either of those things. Harvey Jordan was thirteen years older than Cookie, and he was to his youngest brother a father, a hero and a potential deliverer. By the time Cookie was sixteen, Harvey had done well as a linotype operator at the Roanoke Rapids newspaper, had been off to fight in World War II, and had returned to his linotype work, first in Roanoke Rapids, then in Rocky Mount, then in Norfolk. "I always felt Harvey was going to do something big for me," Cookie says. "I mean, that's the way I felt. He was the one person looking out after me. If any good thing was going to come to me, it was going to come through him, was the way I had always figured it. He just made me feel that way." But in 1952, when Harvey was twenty-nine and Cookie sixteen, the older brother died of leukemia. Looking back, Cookie believes the death of Harvey Jordan was more than the death of a favorite brother. It was an ending of hope.

Cookie spent his four years in the Air Force as a sheet-metal fitter, traveling from base to base in the Orient, adapting new parts to Air Force planes as part of a small team that carried its own welding and machine tools. He liked the work, liked the Air Force, except for the separation from Eloise, whom he saw only on occasional holiday flights home. But he never did anything about it, did not make a career out of it. When he was discharged, in 1958, the Southern California aircraft plants were hiring thousands of workers, and offering high pay. Cookie never applied. When he came home and moved in with Eloise in her parents' home, Cookie heard about jobs in Hampton and Langley, Virginia, near Norfolk, in the aircraft-rocket-space complex there. He never went. Whatever he was waiting for never happened. Whoever he was expecting to take care of things never did.

And while he was waiting, his first child was born: Ina Renee, on April 14, 1956, three days before his first wedding anniversary.

When Cookie Jordan came home from the Air Force in the spring of 1958 and moved in with his wife, daughter and in-laws, he spent the first several days in remote thought. He had to find a job, and, he realized, he had almost limited himself to Roanoke Rapids. And that small choice he had further limited by ruling out the mills. Cookie went to "JP," the name the mill hands gave the new owners when the J. P Stevens chain bought the six Roanoke Rapids mills in 1956, and he was interviewed for a management-trainee job. "If you take a job like that, you got to look down on the workers. You got to be aloof; you got to be above them; you got to be better than they are. I couldn't do that kind of stuff. I just couldn't do it. If I hadda went in there, I woulda quit or they'da fired me one, because I couldn't act like that," he says.

Cookie saw enough, as a child, of the way his mother was scorned and driven by bossmen. He would never do that. He saw enough, as a child, of the way a mill hand lives. "I made up my mind when I was a little bitty fella that I would never work in that mess. I just wouldn't do it. Something better for me than that. I mean anything: working in a service station pumping gas, anything was better than that. I couldn't see myself day in and day out working in that place; couldn't breathe, somebody breathing down your neck all the time. You got to do what they say. I couldn't fight that," he says. No union organizer, no outsider of any kind told Cookie Jordan this. He learned it from his mother, from her fellow workers, and from what he saw growing up in Roanoke Rapids. In the end, he went to work in the paper mill on the riverbank, starting as a general laborer.

In some ways, the Albemarle Paper Manufacturing Company plant is an anomaly in Roanoke Rapids. More than eight hundred men and women work there, and since 1934 about two-thirds of them have been union members. Their wages generally are better, and working conditions better, than those of most of the cotton-mill workers in town. And nearly all the workers at the paper plant live in Roanoke Rapids, in neighborhoods, on streets, next door to the mill hands. But there never has been any move by the paper-plant unionists to convert the mill hands to unionism. The mill hands themselves do not seem to notice any connection between the living standards of the paper-plant workers and their union, and the living standards of the mill hands and their lack of a union. The paper plant seems absorbed by the cotton mills.

Part of this is because the mills employ more than four times as many workers. And part of it is because the paper plant is physically remote, on the northern edge of town at the river's edge, while the mills are scattered through every neighborhood in Roanoke Rapids, are in fact the neighborhood focal points, since each area began as a village constructed by the mill for the mill hands. But most of the explanation for the absence of influence from the paper-plant workers is in fact that from the day Major Emry founded the town to the present ownership by J. P. Stevens, the cotton mills have clutched every shred of power and influence the bossmen and owners could find. They held power not so much maliciously, to deny it to anyone else; nor to use power for the good of the mill hands and the town. They held power over their workers because they feared them.

Soon after he got his job at the paper plant, Cookie Jordan began building a home for his wife and daughter. He used a Veterans' Administration loan to finance $10,500 for a small brick house on the northwest side of town, in a new subdivision less than a mile from the river and from his favorite fishing spot, a jumble of rock and boulder from the power-company dam, a spot called the tail race. The house had two bedrooms and a den, and sat on a corner lot at Pinecrest and Lakey Drive. Eloise, Renee and Cookie had hardly moved in when their troubles surfaced. It began with drinking.

Cookie had not changed, not become a different man or found new parts of himself during his four years in the Air Force. He had not used his years in the Far East to explore an older, foreign culture; he had, instead, kept to the airbases, never leaving the culture he already knew. He might just as well have never left town. Nor had Eloise ventured out of Roanoke Rapids very far or for very long. Now they were four years older than they had been when they married (Cookie was twenty-three, Eloise twenty-two). They had a child. They had not seen much of each other in the past four years. Those things all brought changes with them, but neither Cookie nor Eloise Jordan had changed themselves. And neither, since high school, had come to know well any other man, in Eloise's case, or woman, in Cookie's.

The paper mill runs on shifts around the clock; morning to afternoon, afternoon to midnight, midnight to morning. The workers usually switch shifts every two weeks. When he got off work in the afternoons or at midnight, Cookie began a habit of drinking a few beers with his friends from the plant before going home. And when he was working the midnight-to-morning shift, he spent most of the daylight down at the tail race, casting for rockfish or bream. Eloise, bored with secretarial work, found a new job the year they moved into the new house. She was a stop-checker in the cotton mills, the same production-control job that was the second cotton-mill job Crystal Lee Pulley held in Burlington. When Eloise and Cookie worked the same hours, his mother or hers kept Renee. Eloise did not hold the mill job long. "She got fired a few months later because she kept talking with the people, the workers. You know, just gossip and things," Cookie says. At the paper mill, the shift supervisor asked Cookie to enter the plant apprenticeship program to learn the mechanics of making paper. The program would not have paid much more, but it promised a chance for promotion later, something he would not find as a general laborer. "I told them no, because Eloise and I were having our troubles then," Cookie says.

The two argued over everything in general and nothing in particular, each dissatisfied with the other but unable to confront each other with that. Eloise claimed to suspect Cookie of seeing another woman, a girl they both knew from high school days. Cookie, unlike his father, had nothing of the womanizer in him, and even the most casual pursuit by a woman would only confuse and upset him. But the other woman was a handy topic. So were his flying lessons. He was using the GI Bill to take small-plane lessons, and Eloise said she did not like it. It was too dangerous, she said. Their arguments over that ended when Eloise called the agent who handled Cookie's life insurance, told the agent about the flying lessons, and had the agent call Cookie to warn him that the policy could be canceled, or the premiums increased, if he kept flying.

The marriage was falling apart, and it was clear Eloise already knew that, and Cookie did not. One Wednesday morning when he got off the midnight-to-morning shift, Cookie and two of his friends from the plant began drinking. They were at the home of one of the other men, and an hour went by, then another, without Cookie going home or phoning Eloise. He had been paid that morning, two weeks' wages in his pocket, and although there was nothing in particular he wanted to do, he did not yet want to go home. The three men drank more. They got in a car and rode around Roanoke Rapids, still drinking, until Cookie passed out in the back seat. When he woke up he was in Virginia Beach, outside Norfolk, and it was late afternoon. It was a time of delicious panic for him. He was off work until Friday, so he was not in trouble at the paper plant. But Eloise—Eloise was going to be angry, and Eloise had no idea where he was right now, no idea he was in Virginia Beach. He was Peck's Bad Boy.

Oh, me, he told himself at the beach, Cookie, you've done it again. And he grinned about it. He would not phone Eloise, Cookie decided. Let her wonder what he'd done, where he was. Passing out in the back seat of a car in Roanoke Rapids and waking up in the same car, except on the sand at Virginia Beach, was all the excuse Cookie needed to take that time to escape from the bickering with Eloise, from the boredom of the paper plant, from Roanoke Rapids, where he had spent most of his life and where he supposed he would spend the rest. Cookie and his two friends spent the afternoon drinking beer to cure their hangovers. By the time they felt better they were nearly drunk again, and the three men hopped from bar to bar along the beach until one of them said it was time to go home. When they got back to Roanoke Rapids, Cookie had another hangover.

Instead of facing Eloise with his thick tongue and thicker head, Cookie fell asleep on the living-room couch at his friend's house. He did not phone Eloise. Near midnight he woke up, looked around the darkened room, placed where he was and remembered what he had done, then felt for his wallet. It was gone. Losing two weeks' wages was no joke. Eloise would be furious, and he had nothing to defend himself with. Cookie's friend drove him home before dawn, and Cookie slipped into bed, trying not to awaken Eloise.

Nothing was said the next morning, the next day, that week or the next week about Cookie's absence. Eloise did not even ask for the wages, to buy groceries, to pay the light bill. Still, there were groceries in the kitchen, and the lights were on. Cookie could not steel himself to tell Eloise what had happened, and the longer things went on, apparently without problems, the more inclined Cookie was to believe that losing two weeks' wages was not going to matter. Why that was so he had no idea. Nor did he want to find out. Five weeks after that drunken trip to the beach, Eloise casually said to Cookie one night at home, "I found out where you were that night. I found you on the sofa, and I took your wallet. You never woke up."

Cookie did not question Eloise about her own lack

of questions for him. If he had, he might have begun to suspect that Eloise was too busy to wonder where Cookie went, too busy with someone else.

Before Cookie had left for the Orient while he was in the Air Force—in fact, the week he and Eloise were married—Cookie introduced Eloise to one of his fishing and hunting pals. While Cookie was overseas, the man, his wife and Eloise became friends. When Cookie returned to Roanoke Rapids, the two couples often spent evenings out together, at the movies, at restaurants, and more frequently at dances. The other man, a used-car salesman, still hunted and fished with Cookie, and Cookie thought the foursome were the best of friends.

By this time, soon after they had moved into their new home, Cookie and Eloise's arguments had grown to be real fights, with slaps and fists, scratches and kicks. Cookie valued the time spent fishing or hunting with his old friend, not only as an escape from home, but also an outlet, a sympathetic ear for his tales of Eloise's bickering.

He especially liked the dance nights out. He and the other man wore sport coats and ties, and they were slick-haired from the shower, grinning and shaking hands at the start of the evening. The women were equally self-conscious, wearing high heels and nylons and their best dresses. The two couples drove to a roadhouse that hired a rock-and-roll dance band on weekend nights, or to some private club such as the Moose Lodge that opened up for weekend dances. Once inside, they would take a table, usually a scarred linoleum-topped table, with old stainless-steel kitchen chairs. Eloise and the other woman would sit, and Cookie and the other man would walk to the bar to buy a bucket of ice and some glasses and soft drinks to go with the bourbon or vodka they carried in brown paper bags. Everyone would have a drink, laughing and looking around the dance floor, trying to talk over the sound of the band, and the two couples would change partners for the first few dances.

Then, before he knew how, almost within an hour, Cookie would be drunk. He would not remember having had that much to drink. He would be as certain as a drunk can be that he had had no more drinks than the other three. Yet he would be drunk and they wouldn't be. Soon he would be too drunk to get out of his chair and dance. So his friend would dance with his own wife and with Eloise. Eloise would smile and tell Cookie not to worry. His friend would smile and tease Cookie about not being able to handle liquor, and Cookie would smile back at them both, relieved they were his friends and were not angry about his being drunk again.

Finally Cookie realized he was getting drunk every time they went dancing. It would be early in the evening, and Eloise or his friend, sometimes both of them, would suggest that Cookie go out to the car and sleep. Sometimes Cookie would not make it that far, and have to run to the parking lot or the men's room to be sick with the liquor.

It took Cookie Jordan months to realize what was happening. "What they were doing when they'd pour me a drink, they'd pour me a shot like that, and pour themselves a little bitty one. Then I was out of the way," he says.

Cookie was working the second shift, afternoon to midnight, when he came home from the paper mill one night in August of 1959 to find no one in the house. Cookie went from room to room in the small brick house, turning on lights and looking for a note. There was none. Then he noticed the car was not parked in the driveway. He did not know what to think. But instead of phoning neighbors or relatives to look for his wife and daughter, Cookie went to bed. He was hoping that by the time he awoke, Eloise and Renee would be back from wherever they had gone. But in the morning he was still alone in his house.

He began his search with Eloise's mother. She knew nothing, she said. At midmorning he walked downtown to a window-supply company where Eloise worked as a secretary. She was not there, as she normally would have been, and no one at the office knew why. As he walked out of the building, Cookie looked at the parking spaces on the side. There he found the family car, locked and empty. He used his own set of keys to open the car and drive back to his house. Then he began phoning, careful always to say nothing that would suggest Eloise had disappeared with Renee, or that he knew nothing of their whereabouts. "Have you seen Eloise?" he asked, as though he were searching for her on a minor errand and had seen her about an hour ago. The next day he found Renee, at his sister-in-law's house. But for two weeks, even though he phoned everyone he knew in town, Cookie found out nothing about Eloise. He suspected, from their answers to his questions, that his brother and sister-in-law knew more than they were telling. At the end of the two weeks, when Cookie threatened him, the brother gave in—but all he knew, he said to Cookie, was that Eloise had run off with another man, and the other man was Cookie's fishing and hunting friend, his partying friend, the used-car salesman, who in turn had left his own wife. He did not know where Eloise and the man had gone.

Cookie and Renee moved in with his mother, who could keep the child while he worked, and while he searched. Through September and early October, Cookie, the cuckolded husband, reluctant and ashamed to search openly, became devious, scheming and two-faced, perhaps for the first time in his life. He questioned, and lied to, his friends and acquaintances, and the used-car salesman's friends, none of whom apparently knew anything other than that the man had left town. The search took nearly all his spare time and occupied his thoughts every day. In the middle of October, Cookie came home to his mother's one day and Renee was gone. Eloise had driven by the house that afternoon, stopped the car, called to Renee, and had driven off with the child. He had no idea where they might have gone, but instead of reporting Renee's abduction to the police, Cookie kept up his questioning.

Late that month he was talking with a friend of the used-car salesman, a man who apparently did not know Cookie's wife had left with the salesman, when the friend asked Cookie if he knew how the salesman was getting along in his new job. Cookie tensed. As a known friend of the salesman's, he could not ask what new job, or where. "Yeah, I wonder how he is getting along," Cookie remembers saying. "Well, the motel business must be pretty good up in Chester, being on the turnpike and all," the man said. Chester, Virginia, hardly two hours' drive from Roanoke Rapids, is a small town between Richmond and Petersburg. "What was that motel?" Cookie said, pretending he had just then forgotten it, and the man, who remembered the name, told him.

He had been so clever for so long in his search for Eloise and her lover that to this day Cookie cannot see how he went wrong this close to the end. Perhaps the friend he was talking with sensed something was wrong and phoned the motel in Chester. Perhaps someone else in Roanoke Rapids already knew where Eloise and the man were and was watching Cookie, to send a warning if his search got close. Whatever happened, Cookie sped to his house immediately after the conversation that day, and got his .38 caliber Smith & Wesson revolver from a bureau drawer in the bedroom. He fully intended to murder both Eloise and her lover, he says now. He drove as fast as possible, far over the speed limit, to the motel in Chester. When he got there he identified himself to the desk clerk as an old friend of the man's, from Roanoke Rapids, and the desk clerk said too bad, they had left just two hours before, left permanently, with no forwarding address.

Cookie Jordan drove back to Roanoke Rapids that night, and again he had no idea where his wife, his ex-friend and now his child as well were hiding. Not until late November, shortly before Thanksgiving, did he hear or find anything to lead to the three. Another friend of Cookie's, and of the salesman, came up to Cookie on the street that day. "Say, I ran into your wife in the city the other day," the man said. Surprisingly, in such a small town, even among the circle of their friends and acquaintances, it was not yet common knowledge that Eloise had left Cookie, so Cookie answered, "Is that right?"—again playing the husband who knew generally where his wife was, had perhaps even arranged for the shopping trip with her. But this time the pose was broken. The man said to Cookie, "Yeah, I saw her there. I didn't see you there." It was the first time anyone outside his immediate family had confronted Cookie Jordan with this. He asked the man where he had seen Eloise, and the man named a shopping center in the city.

This time Cookie did not get in his car and race to the city. Instead he phoned an old friend who was a detective on the vice squad of the city Police Department, and he got the friend to search for Eloise and her lover. "I figured she must live near where she shopped," Cookie says. The detective concentrated his search in the neighborhoods around the shopping center. Cookie swore out an arrest warrant, charging Eloise and the salesman with lewd and lascivious behavior and with contributing to the delinquency of a minor. His detective friend called Cookie in early December. He had found Eloise. She was working in a drug store. He had found her lover, too. He was selling cars in the same neighborhood. And he had found their apartment, the second floor of an old frame house. Once again, Cookie loaded his pistol and set out after Eloise.

Cookie reached the city several hours past sunset. He had no trouble following the directions the detective had given him to find the street where Eloise lived. Cookie drove slowly down the street, passed the big house, and parked two blocks beyond it. He shut off the motor and sat a moment, and then got out of the car, quietly closed the door, and walked slowly back up the street. The house was set well back from the street, with large trees and a row of dense bushes in the front yard. Cookie pulled the pistol from his jacket pocket. He checked to see it was fully loaded. Then he crawled into the thickest part of the bushes and hid, in a crouch.

There were no lights on upstairs in the old house. There were lights on in the back, downstairs, but no sounds, no television set, no voices, reached Cookie in the bushes. He thought it likely no one was at home in either apartment. Fifteen minutes passed, and Cookie saw a car pull to the curb in front. Eloise, her lover and Renee got out. They walked up the driveway, passing no more than five feet from Cookie in the bushes, and when they were no more than ten feet beyond him, he leveled his pistol at the man's back.

"I'm going to burn 'em both down," Cookie remembers thinking at that moment. That is the last clear recollection of the night that he has today.

Cookie Jordan cannot explain to himself, he says, why he did not pull the trigger. He did not shoot either of them, did not call out to them from the bushes, did not even rise from the half-crouch he took when he leveled the pistol at the man's back. He watched them until they were out of sight, until they must have gone inside, and then Cookie must have walked back to his car—he does not clearly remember—and either phoned his detective friend or gone to see him. The next morning Eloise and her lover were arrested. Cookie saw her briefly at the police station. He spoke to her once. "The hell with you," he told her. Then he took Renee and returned to Roanoke Rapids. Eloise and her lover were tried and convicted, fined, and ordered not to cohabitate.

Cookie Jordan had been married to Eloise for eight years. They had spent two of those eight years together. "She was a good person when we went together, in school and all. She was a good person. She was fun to be around. She was a real nice person. But the change that come about in her, it still really amazes me. It's just like two different people. I don't know. I'm damn if I've ever been able to figure that out. I couldn't figure it out then, because the things that she did were things that she would never have done—I thought she would never have done. Really. But that's the way it—I don't know. And I didn't beat her and all this kind of stuff. I just didn't do that. I didn't do something I should have done. I don't know what it was, but I didn't do something. Something I did, and something I didn't do too," Cookie Jordan says.

3

ON A HOT, rainy and muggy Saturday in June of 1962, Crystal Lee Wood put her six-month-old son, Jay, in a car seat and buckled two-year-old Mark to a strap in the front seat of her old Buick sedan for the move to Roanoke Rapids. She sang with the radio for most of the three-hour drive, happy to be going and hoping for a fresh start in life, making the same move, in the opposite direction, that Albert Pulley and his family had made seven years earlier.

By the time she turned in the driveway at Syretha and Walter Medlin's home in Roanoke Rapids, Crystal Lee was eager to step into her new life right away. Her sister and brother-in-law were there to greet her. The Medlins had six children, aged sixteen, fifteen, thirteen, eleven, one, and six months, and the thirteen-year-old, a girl, was in the front yard watching the infants in a playpen. Walter took the suitcases inside.

Crystal Lee, not wanting to waste a moment of her new freedom, put Mark and Jay in the playpen and walked in the house to see Walter. He was working second shift at the paper mill that night, three in the afternoon to midnight. It was time for him to leave for work, but before he left, Crystal Lee said to him, "Walter, I want you to bring Cookie Jordan over here tonight for me to meet."

Soon after midnight, Walter came home from work and Cookie Jordan was with him. Cookie wore an old hunting cap, which he kept on inside the house. His face was thin. He had lost so much weight in the months since Eloise had left that he barely filled the gritty work clothes he apologized for wearing. He looked like a man who might swallow himself.

Crystal Lee overwhelmed him. Cookie had seen her only from a distance before, and liked her long, dark hair, her pale face and the curves of her body. "I seen her in the back yard sometimes when she came from Burlington. But I never even dreamed that she and I would end up together. I never even give it a thought," he says. That night the two of them sat in the living room and talked for an hour. Crystal Lee told Cookie she was in Roanoke Rapids to stay. He told her he had sold the brick house behind the Medlins', and he and his daughter now lived with his mother. Crystal Lee invited him for Sunday dinner.

Cookie put on his best suit, and a tie, to call on her the next evening. Walter and Syretha were at church, and Crystal Lee was getting the six Medlin children and the two of her own ready for bed when Cookie rang the doorbell. Crystal Lee put Cookie to work. He took off his coat, rolled up his sleeves and bathed the smaller children. Crystal Lee had spaghetti for him, and the two ate in the kitchen. Cookie washed the dishes while Crystal Lee put the older children to bed. And that was the way their courtship went, dates with the children, his, hers, or the Medlins', for three weeks until they had a night out by themselves.

Crystal Lee had to ask Cookie to kiss her the first time, on that first night out by themselves. She told him then how sad she had been, that she just wanted a home for her children, and a place of her own, away from Albert Pulley. "I could never have any men friends with Daddy," she told Cookie. Years later, remembering that night, Crystal Lee said, "Really, I asked Cookie to marry me. I told Cookie if he would help me, I would help him." That is the way Cookie remembered it: "She and I both needed somebody. She needed a father for her two boys, and I needed a mother for my daughter."

Crystal Lee had a small income then, even though she was not working. She had the settlement money from Jay's father, and monthly social-security payments for Mark after Junior Wood died. Using the settlement money as the down payment, Crystal Lee picked the house she wanted to live in with Cookie. It was a small white slate-shingle house at 61 Carolina Street in Roanoke Park, a quiet neighborhood across town. It had green window shutters, aluminum awnings over the front windows, and a small grove of pecan trees in the back yard. Crystal Lee and Cookie, and sometimes Cookie's mother, spent evenings and days off painting the rooms inside. Crystal Lee and Cookie had decided to marry each other, but they wanted to wait a few months. She wanted to finish fixing the new house the way she wanted it, then move in with her children. They would get married near the end of the year. Cookie's divorce became final that summer, and he began spending weekends, and occasional nights, with Crystal Lee. The arrangement suited them, but it did not please Albert Pulley.

He and Odell were spending a weekend with Crystal Lee when she told him her plans. "I told Daddy that we were going to wait awhile before we got married; that me and the young'uns was going to stay here, and Cookie and me was going to date and get to know each other," she says. Her father opposed her move back to Roanoke Rapids because he considered it "the most gossiping place in the world." And he was angry when she told him her plans now. "I don't want people thinking you are shacking up together. You get married as soon as his divorce comes through," he told Crystal Lee. She did not want any more fights with her father, and she thought Cookie did not care whether they married then or later. That Sunday, after her parents left, Crystal Lee said to Cookie, "Hell, Cookie, let's get married."

This time Albert Pulley did not come to the wedding. No one from Crystal Lee's family did. Syretha and Walter had to work. The thirteen-year-old Medlin girl kept Mark and Jay during the wedding. Neither Cookie nor Crystal Lee were church members, so Cookie's sister, Ernestine, suggested they ask her preacher to marry them, and they did. The ceremony was short. It was in the East Tenth Street Christian Church, and the only ones there were Crystal Lee, Cookie, Ernestine, his mother, Lucy, and the preacher, Clyde Wheeler. After the ceremony, Ernestine and Lucy Jordan went back to their homes, and Crystal Lee and Cookie drove to Syretha's to pick up Mark and Jay. At home, in the house on Carolina Street that night, Crystal Lee phoned Albert Pulley and told him she was married now. He had little to say. There was no honeymoon trip—Cookie wanted to spend that money on the house—and hardly a shift in the routine Crystal Lee and Cookie had had before the wedding. The next morning Cookie went to work as usual at the paper mill. Crystal Lee stayed home, with Mark, Jay and Cookie's daughter, Renee.

It seemed to Crystal Lee that what little romance she and Cookie had had before the wedding evaporated after it. She stayed home almost every day with Mark and Jay, and with Renee as well until the child moved to live with her mother two years later. Crystal Lee did not look for another job. Cookie told her she could not earn enough to pay for a baby-sitter. He was out of the house on most of his days off, fishing and hunting with his friends. He spent on a fishing boat money Crystal Lee wanted to spend on other things. "Junior had taken me to dances all the time. Cookie, I think he took me to one dance. I had thought that maybe we would go dancing sometimes. He had money to spend on his boat, to buy gas, to buy shells, to buy fishing supplies. Because there I was with Mark and Jay, and his daughter too, looking after her. And then he brought his niece in there, who at the time was about fifteen, and she stayed with us some, and I had the responsibility of her," Crystal Lee says. Cookie does not remember it that way. "I spent my time off fooling around the house. I try to keep my house in good shape, the yard and everything, and work on the car, mess with the young'uns," he says.

Soon after Renee moved to her mother's, in 1965, Crystal Lee had her third baby, a girl she and Cookie named Elizabeth. The three children were with her constantly, and she began asking herself what she had been like before she had had any children, a time she could barely remember. Marriage with Cookie had not turned out the way she hoped. He was a father for

Mark and Jay, and because of that she might overlook the dreary nights watching television and the weekends by herself while he went fishing. But Cookie failed her in another way, she believed. He had none of Junior Wood's success, brief though that had been, in keeping Albert Pulley out of her life.

"Daddy came to see the children almost every weekend," Crystal Lee says. "I still felt like Daddy was trying to possess me. And Daddy loved Mark. He would take Mark back to Burlington with him, and I just had to let him do it, and he'd keep him weeks until I had to call up and beg Daddy to bring Mark back. I'd usually end up crying every time. But I didn't want Mark to grow up worshipping his granddaddy like I grew up worshipping my daddy. Cookie never could help me with that. He never pushed Daddy on it the way I asked him to. Cookie would go hunting and fishing all the time, and leave me with all these kids. I was only twenty-five at the time, and it just got to be very boring," she says. Crystal Lee began to see her life and the life around her in Roanoke Rapids in a different way. She thought about things she had not noticed before, the boredom changing her views, so that, for one thing, a man she once considered just a friend now seemed to be something else.

He was a tall, big-boned, fair-haired handsome man, almost twenty years older than Cookie. He seemed to know everyone in town. Almost everyone he knew, Crystal Lee says, feared him. He owned a machine-repair shop and Crystal Lee's father had done business with him when the Pulleys had lived in Roanoke Rapids. It was rumored in town that the man also had a hand in some shady operations, selling benzedrine pills, running high-stakes card games, distributing pornographic films. Cookie also knew the man, Ira

Stonehouse,* and got to know him better when he married Crystal Lee. Stonehouse and his wife lived near the Jordans on Carolina Street, and the big man often came by for coffee. Cookie did not like him, in part because of the rumors, but mostly because Stonehouse was the town rake, a ladies' man. Crystal Lee knew Cookie did not like Ira. But Stonehouse ignored Cookie, joking and smiling, winking at Crystal Lee. Cookie kept his dislike to himself, smiling back and quietly going off to hunt or fish with Stonehouse whenever the man asked him.

"Just before I married Cookie, I was sewing these curtains, and Ira would come by and talk to me. Cookie didn't like him because Ira was a woman's man, and he didn't do right by his children, moneywise. His wife always bitched to him. But people have reasons for being what they are. Ira would come and he'd sit there and talk while I sewed. And I liked him then, but he never made a pass at me. He never did after all the things I'd heard about him. Before I married Cookie, he never made a pass, but I just considered him a friend of mine," Crystal Lee says. Cookie always took the car to work with him and took it hunting or fishing on his days off, and Stonehouse always offered one of his cars whenever Crystal Lee complained that Cookie had theirs. Mark had developed an allergy, a racking cough that often required immediate medical attention, and there were many times that Crystal Lee borrowed a car from Stonehouse to take Mark to the doctor. He told her once to keep it as long as she wanted.

"One Saturday, I had taken Mark to the doctor, and I stopped by and got Ira, and he came over to the

*Not the man's real name.

house, and he could tell that I was very unhappy. I was concerned because there Mark was, one of my children was sick again. Cookie was down on the river somewhere, fishing. We were talking, and he propositioned me then. He said that he wouldn't get me in any trouble. He said that, you know, we could go out to dinner sometimes; that anything I wanted I could have. And I said, 'Well, I'll think about it.' So it was coming up to be around Eastertime, and my cousin and I, we were very close, and I told her. She said, 'Well, hell, Lee, you unhappy anyway. Why don't you take him up on it?' Said, 'It might help your marriage,'" Crystal Lee says.

A few days later Ira Stonehouse suggested a shopping trip to Richmond. They could go on a Saturday and be back that night, he said. He asked Cookie to come along. Cookie wanted to go fishing instead. Crystal Lee's cousin kept Mark, Jay and Elizabeth, and Ira and Crystal Lee went to Richmond for the day. "I told him on the way up to Richmond that I didn't see where having an affair could do any harm. I said, 'As long as you understand it won't be a permanent thing. I don't want any of this you falling in love with me, or me falling in love with you.' I mean, I really sounded tough, but found out I was very weak after all, and so was he. But, I mean, he loved to dance. There he was. I mean, he was a very handsome man, you know, and I just fell head over heels in love with him, really. And he did me too," Crystal Lee says. Her affair with Stonehouse continued for nearly three years, until one weekend when Crystal Lee was in Burlington visiting her parents.

She was driving alone, taking a ride through town, when she found herself passing the home of Miles Simmons' parents. Crystal Lee knew from her high school friends that her former lover was a wealthy young man now. He had finished college and graduated from law school, and was married and living in a small town in western North Carolina. Her friends told her Simmons and his family lived in a big house, one with chandeliers and circular stairs to the front porch, and Crystal Lee often wondered how life might have been if she and her sons lived in that house, and had that much money. Simmons' old convertible, the one he had had in college, was parked at his parents' home when Crystal Lee drove by and saw it. "I called and I asked for him, and I told him that if he wanted to see his son he could come over and see him now, or I'd bring him. He said no, that under the circumstances he thought it would be better for him and the child if they never saw each other," Crystal Lee says. The rejection hurt her, and the memories of her affair with Simmons joined her thoughts of the affair she was having with Ira Stonehouse.

Cookie did not know Stonehouse and Crystal Lee were lovers, and after that trip to Burlington, in the fall of 1968, Crystal Lee hoped to end the affair before he found out. She could not bear the guilt she had begun to feel, nor what she saw in herself when she thought of Simmons and Stonehouse. She tried going to church, hoping that would give her the determination to break off with Stonehouse. "But I knew people knew these things, and people gossiped, and I couldn't be a hypocrite. I couldn't go to church with them thinking that," she says.

Crystal Lee avoided Stonehouse for several weeks. She began to hope the affair would wither away, and Cookie would never know—if she ended it herself she feared Stonehouse, in anger, might confront Cookie with the story. "See, Ira had money, and he had always been used to getting what he wanted. I think when I just said no, this life is not for me, is not what I want for my children, he couldn't take it. He just didn't believe that I had let him down. He was used to always putting the woman down, where I actually put him down," Crystal Lee says.

She was sitting up late one night, after midnight—the children were asleep and Cookie was gone, working the midnight-to-morning shift at the paper mill—when Stonehouse knocked on the front door. Crystal Lee smelled liquor on the big man's breath. She did not know if she should let him in the door. Stonehouse smiled at her and said, "Where you been, honey? You haven't been coming to see me." If he was smiling, perhaps she could tell him now, Crystal Lee thought: keep it light, make a joke of it all, and send him away. She let him inside, and they sat in the living room. But Crystal Lee found she was too frightened to joke. All she could tell Stonehouse was how bad their affair made her feel, how she feared Cookie would learn of it sooner or later, and that she was ending it now. There would be no last kiss, nothing, she told him. "Just leave," she said. Stonehouse had not said a word. He stood up, walked to her chair, drew his huge hand back, and slapped her across the face. The single blow knocked Crystal Lee to the floor. Lying there, she watched Stonehouse turn away and walk out the front door.

When Cookie came home from work, Crystal Lee told him what had happened. She told him about her affair with Stonehouse. She said she wanted Cookie to hear it from her first. She said Stonehouse had been trying to corner her the past few weeks, following her downtown, surprising her in stores, coming by the house when Cookie was at work, and she was afraid he would keep chasing her now. She asked Cookie to forgive her, and protect her from Stonehouse, and with hardly a word of anger, Cookie said he would. Crystal Lee did not tell him how or why she began the affair, and Cookie did not ask.

It was late in the morning when Crystal Lee and Cookie finished talking. Cookie got up from the kitchen table where they sat and walked to the bedroom. He got his pistol from a bureau drawer, the same .38-caliber Smith & Wesson revolver he had taken to Norfolk in search of his first wife and her lover, and he walked out the front door. Crystal Lee saw the pistol in his jacket pocket. She did not try to stop him.

Cookie drove to Stonehouse's machine shop. He parked in front, got out of the car, and walked toward the office. His hand was inside his pocket, gripping the pistol, when one of the mechanics came out of the office door and saw him. Cookie asked for Stonehouse. The mechanic said Stonehouse was out of town for the day on a business trip. "I really wasn't planning on doing anything to him," Cookie said later, remembering that day. "I had gone to warn him away from my wife, and I took my pistol because I figured he might have one on him too," he said. Cookie drove back home. He told Crystal Lee that Stonehouse was out of town. She wanted to go to the police, to see Drewery Beale, chief of police in Roanoke Rapids, and the husband of her first cousin. It was a difficult story to tell, she said, but perhaps Chief Beale could keep Stonehouse away from them.

Beale was a casual-appearing man, quiet, soft-spoken, with the size and build of a man who might have been a star end in high school football, once rangy and broad-shouldered, now putting on weight. They met in his office. Beale sat quietly, looking without nodding or talking. Crystal Lee felt guilty and ashamed telling him her story. She wanted to spill out every detail just to fill the silence she thought Beale would let drag on if she stopped talking. The chief knew from his wife about Crystal Lee's affair with Miles Simmons, and the birth of Jay. Knowing he knew that made it harder for Crystal Lee to talk about Stonehouse and persuade Beale to issue a peace warrant against her ex-lover. "I guess Drewery Beale thought that I was a two-bit whore, so why should I get any consideration? But a two-bit whore needs help, and she should get justice from a police department. They're supposed to treat a two-bit whore just the way they do a doctor's wife. A two-bit whore has a mental problem. She needs help more than the doctor's wife," Crystal Lee says. Ira Stonehouse never bothered Crystal Lee again. He died three years later in a state hospital for alcoholics, when his liver failed.

"Well, after that happened, things seemed to be real good," Cookie says. "We forgave each other for what we had done, decided to pick up the pieces and really make it work. And there for a while, it really seemed that it was going to work. We got along good. Things improved financially. We could do the things we wanted to do. We could provide better for the kids," he says.

Cookie had misjudged his marriage, though, and things only seemed to be real good. Crystal Lee had not, perhaps could not, explain to Cookie how she felt about him, about her father, about herself and any man. Cookie, in turn, had not explained to Crystal Lee, perhaps not to himself either, how he felt when he compared his first marriage to his second, when he thought of the affair with Stonehouse, and the affair with Simmons. Their mutual forgiveness was meant by each to encompass all that had happened, what they had spoken of, and what they had not. As a result, the forgiveness covered nothing.

Cookie adopted Jay soon after this. He laughed when the county welfare department told him their social workers had to approve him formally as a suitable father for Jay. And though it angered Cookie, he kept his feelings to himself when Albert Pulley opposed the adoption. "He didn't ever want me to have full control over those children, because after all, they're not my children, and I shouldn't be given all the authority of a father. That's what he thought, and that burnt my ass, right there. It always did gall me. The way I feel about it, if I'm going to pay for this boy's education, if I'm going to pay for the clothes on his back, if I'm going to feed him, clothe him, I'm gonna have a say-so in what he does. Now I want my children to go to school, because I want better for them than what I had. But, you know something else? Young boys coming up now have everything in the world going for them. I never did," Cookie says. He never mentioned his feelings about Mark and Jay to Crystal Lee.

There was much in her thoughts that Crystal Lee never mentioned to Cookie either. "Maybe it was because of the closeness between me and my daddy, but for some reason I've always felt like I've always wanted to help men, all men, and all boys. For some reason. I don't know. I've always had this feeling. Like, you take a man that you see that might be worried about something. It seems like that I just want to try and talk to him. And that's so strange about me and Cookie. I just never have really wanted to help Cookie. Cookie always seemed like the kind, he had his own mind, and no matter what I said to him, it was wrong anyway. He's accused me of always trying to help other people, and never helping him," Crystal Lee says. "I don't know. I've always liked men better than I do women. A lot of women that I ever came in contact with, mothers or whatsoever, I know I've always spoke my mind. And I used to be a flirt, and I guess maybe I still am a flirt, really. Women naturally don't like these things, and they always sort of look down on me because of them," she says.

Through 1968 and 1969, Crystal Lee resumed her routine of housekeeping and raising her children. She avoided other men. She missed working, though—she had not worked since Junior Wood's death in early 1961. There was Mark to look after, then Jay, then the move to Roanoke Rapids, then marriage to Cookie, and for a time the responsibility of his daughter from his first marriage, and then the birth of Elizabeth. Each of these seemed to her to come one right after the other. She no more reached the verge of adjusting to one child when along came another, or along came a new marriage, or a move. Even the affair with Ira Stonehouse seemed to her, looking back at it, to be another thing in the list of things that kept her from sitting down and deciding whether or not there was anything else she wanted to do.

She did not want to work in the cotton mills again, but even that would be some job, something not just to get her out of the house, but to help her feel better about herself. Cookie's opposition prevented her from doing much about it. "Tell you the truth, I didn't ever like the damn idea of her working to start with," Cookie would say later. "She brought in extra money, that's true. But yet, it took more money for her to work: extra clothes she had to have, eating out more often. Really, in the long run, we didn't benefit financially all that much. I didn't feel like we did. But she likes to feel she is contributing just as much as I am, which she was when she went to work. But her contribution to the marriage I wanted to be as a home-builder, in the home. And far as her having outside activities, being in clubs and such as that, I never had any objections to that. I never objected at all."

The cotton mills were always there, and Crystal Lee knew she could work them. She had as a teen-ager, had again when she married Junior Wood; she had lived with the cotton mills all her life. Crystal Lee grew up knowing, as every mill hand and bossman knew, that if you couldn't find something better, and you almost never could, it did not take much to get hired at the mills.

She tried to find something better. In 1969 a new vocational-education school, the Halifax County Technical Institute, opened on the outskirts of Roanoke Rapids. Cookie agreed to let her take two courses. He changed his mind about her working. "We got by for a right good while with just me working. But as the family grew, and the cost of living grew, we just needed more," he says. Crystal Lee took a waitress training course. Syretha was head waitress at a large motel restaurant, in addition to working in one of the cotton mills, and Crystal Lee hoped her sister could get her a job. In case Syretha could not, Crystal Lee took a second course, power sewing. That course might get her a job in an apparel plant, she thought, which was still better than working in a cotton mill.

The waitress course lasted two weeks. It was held in a motel restaurant, and at the end of the course, Crystal Lee was offered a job in a motel restaurant, a motel where tourists from the North spent the night on their way south to Florida. "You can make good money in the summertime as a waitress," Crystal Lee says. For three weeks she did, while she stuck with the power sewing class at nights just in case. The restaurant work was hard. She had to rush through every day's shift to keep pace with the flow of hungry tourists. There was a flow of tips, though, and Crystal Lee thought she would like the job. Working again suited her. She was seeing, talking with, someone other than Cookie, Mark, Jay and Elizabeth. She even liked the way she looked in her waitress uniform. It was short-skirted, a little tight around her breasts, and clean and crisp. To her the uniform was only slightly provocative. Wearing it made her feel more pert and perky than sexy. But her boss, the manager of the restaurant, did not think the same. He found Crystal Lee attractive not only to himself but also to some of his customers, businessmen who stayed regularly at the motel, and who had learned that the restaurant sometimes had waitresses available for dates, for a price.

The manager called Crystal Lee aside one afternoon after her shift. He told her what he had in mind, how much more money she could make, how much fun she could have. It was not just any motel guest, he said, but only the important ones, VIPs who would be sure to show her a good time, take her out dining and dancing beforehand. She could say yes or no to each before going out, the manager said. Crystal Lee did not say yes or no to her boss. She did not come back to work the next day. By the end of that week, Syretha found Crystal Lee a job in the restaurant where she worked.

It was Crystal Lee's first full-time job in nearly nine years, and she liked it. She worked at the restaurant through the summer and fall, rotating her shifts with

Cookie's hours at the paper mill so one of them could be home with the three children. In November she spent Thanksgiving with Albert and Odell in Burlington. They made plans then for the Pulleys to spend Christmas in Roanoke Rapids. Albert and Odell would drive over on Christmas Eve and stay with Crystal Lee and Cookie. Crystal Lee waited at home Christmas Eve night. The tree was trimmed, and there were presents under it. Midnight passed without a sign, not even a phone call, from Albert and Odell. At one o'clock Christmas morning, Crystal Lee phoned her parents in Burlington. Odell Pulley answered the phone. She began to cry when she recognized her daughter's voice.

"Momma said Daddy hadn't been out of the house since Thanksgiving," Crystal Lee says. "She said he was real sick, but she couldn't get him to the hospital, or the doctor. He just wouldn't listen to Momma, and Momma was afraid to call me because my daddy was right there in the house and he might hear her," she says. Crystal Lee told Cookie she would have to go to Burlington herself to make Albert Pulley see a doctor. She would leave that morning, and call Cookie from Burlington. At five o'clock on Christmas morning she phoned Syretha at the restaurant—Syretha was working the early shift. Crystal Lee told her what their mother said. "The men are going to have to keep the children, and you and I go to Burlington right away," Crystal Lee said. They took the Jordan car and were in Burlington before noon.

"Daddy looked so gray. And he looked like he hadn't shaved since Thanksgiving," Crystal Lee says. When he saw her, Albert Pulley grinned at his daughter, and he told her, "Honey, you getting too fat." Crystal Lee laughed. She told him she knew it. "He was in the bed, and I had his presents with me, and when I gave them to him he just laid them on the bed. He just was not himself." She walked out of the bedroom. Odell stood in the hallway, outside the door. "Momma was still afraid he would get mad, so she was whispering to me to call the doctor," Crystal Lee says.

The two women went in the kitchen. Crystal Lee began searching for the family doctor by phone. She had to dial a dozen or more numbers before she found the doctor. While she dialed she recalled Albert Pulley's last visit to Roanoke Rapids. It was two weeks before last Thanksgiving, and Pulley had made a point of seeing all his sisters, brothers and cousins in town. He had even had Crystal Lee drive him sixty miles north into the Virginia countryside to spend an hour with one favorite cousin. "He knew he was dying, I guess," Crystal Lee says. Looking out the kitchen window as she called all over Burlington for the doctor, Crystal Lee saw snow falling. It was the first white Christmas in Burlington in years, and the sight brought to mind her memories of Albert Pulley slipping away from the mills and coaxing his favorite daughter to stay home from work so they could play in the snow.

Pulley heard her on the phone. "Honey, you giving that phone hell, ain't you?" he shouted from his bed. "Yeah, Daddy, I'm gonna get you in the hospital before this day's over," Crystal Lee said. "No, you ain't," he said.

When the doctor arrived and examined Albert Pulley, he told him he had to get to the hospital immediately. "Daddy said he wouldn't go, and I just said me and the doctor would carry him out if he didn't. We had to hold him up anyway. He fell down walking out the door, and the doctor took him by one arm and I got the other, and we got him in the car," Crystal Lee says.

Crystal Lee phoned Cookie from the hospital. She would not be home for Christmas, she said, and she asked him to phone the rest of the Pulley family in Roanoke Rapids and tell them about her father. She phoned her younger sister, Geraldine, and told her, and then she left the hospital. She drove through Burlington alone, past the Pulleys' first home there, past her old high school, the florist shop downtown, the apartment she and Junior Wood shared, the two cotton mills, Haw River and Glen Raven, where she had worked as a child, and out to Swepsonville, past the intersection where Junior was killed. That night the doctor told her Albert Pulley's kidneys were irreparably damaged. He had an enlarged heart as well, the doctor said, and it was a question of which would kill him first. "The doctor said Daddy's getting worse, he's not getting better. 'Honey, your daddy's dying,' is what he said," Crystal Lee remembers.

Crystal Lee and Odell sat by Albert Pulley's bed, one on each side, for most of the day after Christmas and the next day. "Daddy hardly recognized me, and I don't think he knew what we were saying to him," Crystal Lee says. On the 27th of December, when she walked into his hospital room that afternoon, Crystal Lee thought her father recognized her. "He started humming 'Jingle Bells,' and I sang along with him. I sang the words," she says. "Momma was holding one hand, and I had his other hand. He pulled me to him, and he said, 'I want to tell you something.' I thought I knew what he was going to say, so I just said, 'Daddy, I know it.' And I went out in the hall to the nurses' station, and Geraldine had just come in the room, and she ran out of it. She was screaming. I went back in his room, and I looked at him, and I said, 'He's dead.' "

Crystal Lee picked out the coffin and she found the

gravesite she wanted for her father. "Daddy always said that when he died he wanted to be buried in Roanoke Rapids. And he is," she says. Crystal Lee chose a plot near the east entrance to Cedarwood Cemetery, on the northern edge of rows of tombstones, on the slope of a hill that overlooks the Roanoke River and the rapids Albert Pulley used to fish. She bought a pale-gray granite marker and had it engraved with the name Pulley. An open Bible crossed by a spray of flowers was engraved at one end of the stone, and under that the quotation, "God is our refuge and strength." When the funeral was over, Crystal Lee stayed behind after her mother, sisters and brother, and Albert Pulley's friends and relatives left. She wanted to make sure the gravediggers covered the coffin with a truckload of white sand she had ordered. "I just couldn't stand the thought of dirt going over him like that," she says. Crystal Lee keeps a spray of plastic flowers on the grave, puts fresh flowers on it on religious holidays, and every year she sows grass seed around her father's grave.

Albert Pulley's death, says Crystal Lee, made her think again about going to church. "Things was going pretty good for me. I was trying to lead a decent, straight life. It's hard to be a Christian. It's easier to be a sinner. But if I'm going to do something, I'm going to be one hundred percent or not at all. So I started going to church every time the door was open," she says.

Crystal Lee went alone, to Calvary Baptist on the Weldon Road a few blocks east of the motel restaurant where she worked. It was as much a meeting hall as a church. Services were more like Alcoholics Anonymous than worship, except these sinners gave their full names. When she started going, there was a preacher named Shotwell who scourged his flock with swirling arms and a screaming promise of eternal damnation. This bawl-and-stomp fundamentalism was, to Crystal Lee, just what she deserved. Everything in her life struck her as a sin she had committed, and she was ready to take the blame for it, accept the guilt. Would Junior Wood have died if she had not fought with him and separated? Would Jay be better off if she had married his father? There was her father: if she had stayed in Burlington instead of moving back to Roanoke Rapids to please only herself, she thought, perhaps she could have coaxed Albert Pulley into a hospital earlier, and saved his life. And there was her affair with Ira Stonehouse.

The first Sunday she went to Calvary Baptist, Crystal Lee felt the hall filled with exorcised sins, beaten out by Preacher Shotwell. "There they were, the people, standing up there and testifying as to sins, and what God had did for them. I went up. I told my story of what I wanted to be," she says. To Preacher Shotwell and his flock she gave every detail. No guilt-ridden harlot was more ready than she to confess her sins to a vengeful Father in Heaven. But Crystal Lee never got another chance after that first week. Preacher Shotwell left town, Calvary Baptist gave up revivals and testimonials, and Crystal Lee stopped going to church.

Her waitress job began to bore her, and she began to complain about the unpredictability of her wages. Some weeks tips were high, some weeks they were low, and there was no predicting either. For a few weeks, in 1971, she quit the restaurant to see what a change would bring. She found a job as a power sewer, first in an apparel plant thirty miles from town, then, a few weeks later, in another apparel plant twenty miles from town. The work was hard, and the drive was long, but the pay was more than she made as a waitress, including tips. She might have stayed with the job, but one afternoon while driving back to Roanoke Rapids from work she saw the car in front of her begin swerving over the highway. It left the road and rolled over and over. Three of her friends from the apparel plant were in that car, and one of them died in the wreck. Crystal Lee was so shaken that the next day she quit her job. She got her waitress job back, and began catering at country-club parties for the restaurant. She felt uncomfortable at those country-club banquets. The feelings from her childhood—that she was not as good as the people who joined country clubs—bothered her. Some nights at the country club she saw the same man, now an important boss at the mills, who years ago had told Albert Pulley to keep his son away from the bossman's daughter. "I saw him looking at me lots of times, and I knew what he wanted from me, too. But he never got close to it," Crystal Lee says.

One day that fall Syretha mentioned that an old friend of the family now worked in personnel for J. P. Stevens, and that started Crystal Lee thinking again about going back to the cotton mills.

It was not that work in the cotton mills was easier than the restaurant, nor that it paid more. It was harder work, she knew from experience, and the wages, while predictable, were not better than her worst weeks in the restaurant and not nearly as good as those weeks when tips were high. Cookie's wages from the paper plant that year, before taxes, were $9,600, and even though she made a dollar and sixty-five cents an hour less than her husband, her family needed her mill wages. Crystal Lee felt comfortable in the mills. Most of her friends, and almost every one of her neighbors, worked there. She was born to working in the mills, she thought. Her father had worked the mills, and her mother still did. Her brothers and sisters did. Cookie's entire family did. She put in an application with the family friend, and after weeks of waiting, on February 2, 1972, she got her first job with JP.

She went to work on the third shift, midnight to eight in the morning, folding fancy towels and washcloths in the gift-sets section of the put-up department at Delta #4 Fabricating Plant. One week later she was transferred to the second shift, four in the afternoon to midnight. For the next eight months, Crystal Lee made two dollars and eighteen cents an hour, standing at a wide table eight hours a night, five and sometimes six nights a week, folding towels. When there were no towels to fold and the bossmen told her to fold napkins, or tablecloths, it did not surprise her that they always kept her busy. Nor did it surprise her when her woman friends in the mill warned her about JP—told her, for one thing, that JP would not take a woman's word for it if menstrual cramps pained her so that she had to sit and rest for a while, or take a shift off. She had to have a physician's note to do that.

Her best friend at work was a young woman, Liz Johnson, who stood at a folding table next to Crystal Lee. Liz was ten years younger, only twenty-two then. She had three children, was divorced, and lived with her parents. Liz introduced Crystal Lee to two other young women, Blondie and Jeannie, who had been in the Women's Army Corps together. Blondie was a slender, pale girl. She was a terry hemmer, but she bore no physical marks of her work, which was sewing hems in terrycloth towels—a sit-down job that eventually shapes a body like a pear. Blondie's friend, Jeannie, was a solid, muscular young woman. She worked as a bar tacker, sewing labels on towels, and as a service worker, a general laborer who pushes and pulls chest-high handtrucks of terrycloth towels from cutter to hemmer to tacker across the wide floor of the fabricating department. The two girls lived together in a trailer on the edge of town.

Some nights during the summer of 1972, Crystal Lee joined her new friends when the shift ended at midnight and drove past Blondie and Jeannie's trailer to a small Air Force radar station a few miles from town. There was an NCO club at the base, and Liz liked to dance with the airmen there. The four women could buy mixed drinks at the NCO club—something which was illegal everywhere in the state except on military bases—and the drinks cost only forty cents each. Cookie never complained about those nights out—he had found a new interest that kept him out some nights on his own. He had found politics, and joined a "political club."

"Boy, that was an outfit in this world, I'm telling you," Cookie says. "What it all stemmed from, the state senator, he was trying to stimulate interest in his campaign. His handyman gets things going by organizing this club. It was at the time when they were having all those riots in New Jersey and all up North. Black people were just stealing everything that wasn't tied down. They were taking it all. Well, Lyles believes on the idea that they were going to happen here, right away. And it was a march planned for Roanoke Rapids, some kind of freedom march for the black people, and we just got to talking. And I said, 'Well, I'll be damn if I'm gonna let 'em tear up what little mess I got. I just ain't gonna let nobody tear it up,' " Cookie says.

"So we got to talking and got together on the thing.

We were gonna help each other, see. They had it rigged up where I had two telephone numbers, and if I needed any help, they could call the rest of them. They had it worked out where if you needed any help, they would be at your house within ten minutes," Cookie says. The group called itself "The Young Men's Club," and the plan Cookie described was a contingency plan for race war in Roanoke Rapids. He said little to Crystal Lee about the group. When she pressed him to explain what he was doing out those nights, he said he had joined a political group he described to her as "just a bunch of the boys getting together." He was cautious with Crystal Lee about the club because the two of them felt differently about race. "I mean, it's not a put-on feeling she has," Cookie says of Crystal Lee. "It's honest. My daughter, Elizabeth, she's colorblind. She doesn't see no color at all, and that is coming from her mother. I know it is."

By August of that year, Crystal Lee once again had grown restless and bored. She did not like the job at the mill. Eight hours of standing and folding towels was drab compared to the casual routine of her old waitress and catering jobs. She thought the mill work was what bothered her, that alone, and on September 2 she quit JP to be a hostess at a new private club in town. It was named the Executive Club, and its members Crystal Lee described as being "bossmen and lawyers." Her hours were four in the afternoon to midnight. She wore her best clothes every night, and looked her best, long hair down to her shoulders, pale face more striking than before with deeply mascara'd eyes and dark lipstick, and her full figure riper and lusher, she thought, in the dim lights of the club. She had never held a job like this, and she liked it.

The club was in a shopping center on East 10th

Street, at one end of the huge blacktop parking lot edged by one-story buildings. On one side of the club's front door was a barber shop, and on the other a television-repair shop. There was a machine on the door into which club members inserted a plastic card that set off a buzzer and unlocked the door. Inside was a beer bar, where set-ups of mixer, ice and glasses were also sold, as were sandwiches, snacks and slices of pizza. Members brought their own liquor bottles with them. Crystal Lee's job was to see that the waitresses kept up with the tables, the bar had enough supplies, the jukebox enough new songs, and the clientele, which was almost entirely male, was happy. It was the kind of place and the kind of job guaranteed to make Cookie Jordan, who had quit smoking and drinking when Eloise left him, angry and jealous.

"Cookie kept telling me, 'Honey, that is no place for you. I just don't want you out there. But you gonna have to try it anyway.' So he let me," Crystal Lee said. Soon after she started working at the club, Crystal Lee and Cookie began arguing about her job. Cookie complained to her many nights. "I didn't like that; I didn't like that at all," he says. "I didn't feel like that was the place for her, to be a barmaid. And that's exactly what it come to, the job she was working. She liked to meet people, and to her, it was all right. I mean she didn't see no harm to it. It's all in the way you look at things, I'm sure, but to me, it was wrong for her to be working there and I told her that. I didn't like the idea worth a damn," he says.

There were nights that fall when Crystal Lee came home after midnight, sleek and alluring in her hostess dress, to find Cookie home from the paper mill, waiting for her at the kitchen table, and still wearing his grimy work clothes. They would have coffee together, and Crystal Lee would drop a hint, with a pout, that one man or another had made a pass at her that night and she really was tired of that and she just wished the men would leave her alone.

Cookie would get angry and jealous. He would tell Crystal Lee he had warned her not to work in the club in the first place, but, no, she had not listened to him. Crystal Lee would shrug it off, tell Cookie it was not that bad, that she did not see what he was so upset about, and he was probably just jealous. She would leave the kitchen and watch the late show on television, or go to bed and fall asleep, leaving Cookie to sit with his anger.

On October 4, after a month of arguing with Cookie, Crystal Lee gave in to him and quit the hostess job. She went back to JP, to the same job, folding towels eight hours a day in the gift-sets department. She hated to give up the hostess job, and was angry with Cookie for making her do it, and with herself for agreeing to. She hated to return to the cotton mill, and she dreaded the malaise that filled her waking moments now. Cookie said of Crystal Lee in those days, "Hell, she didn't have to do that. She didn't have to work at all. I made enough. But there again, she felt like that it was important that she do this. It was important to her. Why, I'll be damned if I'll ever know."

4

CRYSTAL LEE did not wear a dress to work now. She put on slacks every day, often the same pair from one day to the next. She wore old shirts, old slacks, old loafers, and the only part of her dress that recalled the Executive Club hostess was her makeup. She did not give up that: lipstick and dark eye liner.

She had to buy a rug, about three feet square, to put on the concrete floor she stood on in the fabricating department in Delta #4 mill. The rug put a little cushion between the concrete and her legs, but her shins still hurt at the end of an eight-hour shift of standing at her table folding towels.

At least she was not working in the weave rooms, she often told herself. Next door to the fabricating mill was Rosemary mill, where many of Crystal Lee's friends worked. In that mill, taking form thread by thread in the weave room, there were richly brocaded cloths for the dining-room tables of the Hilton Hotels and the Americana of Miami Beach. Rows and rows of old wooden looms roared like waterfalls and shook the floors with a constant trembling vibration the weavers soaked up through the legs, disorienting their vision and balance. No one talked because no one could hear. Steam vents spewed mist into every corner of the huge weave room to keep the yarn hot (80 degrees) and wet (65 percent humidity) for the best weaving. Mosquito netting rose from the floors and disappeared overhead in the high dark reaches toward the ceiling, netting to keep flying lint off—not off the weavers, but off the different kinds and colors of tablecloths made on the same open floor.

Weavers say things could be worse. In the cotton mills, the thing to do is keep away from what they call the raw, to get a job as far down the manufacturing process as possible from that point where the cotton bales are brought into the mills. At that point are stationed the hopper feeders, all of them men, who spend eight hours a day breathing through surgical masks that cover their noses and mouths, ripping apart bales of cotton, feeding them into the mouths of hoppers, machines that shred cotton fibers and rip them apart.

Next to a hopper feeder's job, the worst is a picker's —the second step in the manufacturing process—and then a carder's in the carding room. All through the mill, cotton dust and lint fill the air and go up the nose and down the throat, into eyes, coating hair from the hopper loaders to the pickers, from the carders to the spinners and doffers. After each step the air gets a little cleaner, but the lint and dust can kill, and do, through a respiratory disease the mill hands call "brown lung" and doctors call byssinosis.

The mill where Crystal Lee worked, Delta #4, was not so dangerous. There was lint in the air, but not as much as in the weave rooms. By the time cloth reached Delta #4 it was nearly through the long process that begins with the hopper feeders. Most of Crystal Lee's working companions were women, and they held simple jobs given simple names: side hemmers, who sew hems in the sides of an unbroken strip of terrycloth toweling; terry loaders, who stand for eight hours a shift taking terrycloth towels from a conveyor belt and loading them on moving racks at the mouth of a drying oven three times their height.

Crystal Lee's folding table was at one end of the shearing room in Delta #4. The room was as big as a pasture. It had no interior walls, and from her table Crystal Lee often looked up and across the room, daydreaming while her hands automatically, routinely, folded towels. She thought about what she did as little as possible: fold, fold, turn, fold, fold, box, fold, fold, turn. There were millions of towels, and no possibility of getting ahead of the flow. Even if she could speed her folding, the bossmen would merely increase the flow of towels to her. And if by sheer oversight that did not happen, and she found herself idle for a few minutes, there would be no one to talk with, since everyone else working with Crystal Lee had her own flow of towels to keep packaging. At the far end of the shearing room, she could see a permanent haze made by lint coming off rolls of terrycloth. The rolls, high as a man, slowly unwound behind the backs of the side hemmers, passing yard by yard through the women's sewing machines. From there, the ribbon of terrycloth, now hemmed on the sides, wound still unbroken to the terry cutters, most of them men, who sliced the ribbon into individual towels with hand-held circular power saws. The cut towels were rolled in huge bins to the terry hemmers, all women, who sewed in end hems and labels, and from there, again in huge rolling bins, the towels went to packaging in the put-up department, of which Crystal Lee's section, gift sets, was a part.

In December, Crystal Lee fractured a small bone when a bin of terrycloth towels rolled over her foot. The accident kept her out of work until the middle of the following April, 1973. In another town, Crystal Lee might have looked for another job during those four months she was out of the mill. In Roanoke Rapids, however, there was almost noplace else to look. Because of Cookie's objections, she could not return to the Executive Club. In winter and early spring, when few tourists were traveling on the interstate highway, the restaurants had no openings for waitresses. The apparel plants were too far away, few of her friends worked there, and she was still afraid of the daily drive. For one reason or another, she always returned to the cotton mills, had done so since she had been a teen-ager in Burlington. She felt powerless to change that pattern in her life, and just as powerless to change anything at all—the dust and lint, the low pay and long hours, the contempt from the bossmen—inside a cotton mill. She lived the way she did because the mills never gave her time or money enough to find anything better. Or was it the other way, that the cotton mills were the only place anyone who lived the way Crystal Lee had could find a job? She did not know which was true, but she often thought about the mills and her life during those four months of idleness. And sometimes she thought it might be inevitable that her children would follow her into the cotton mills. She feared that, and so did Cookie; he knew how easy it would be for the mills to swallow up Mark and Jay and Elizabeth. "They been raised just like I was, same story over and over. They have, JP has, in a way, brainwashed the parents: they wore out. All their life, all the children ever hear is JP. The parents come home and say, 'Lord a mercy, they worked me down today.' They say the weave room this, or spinning room this, or card room this. That's all the children have heard. So naturally they're going to pick it up, learn about it. And they going to work for JP. JP wants to get the family into the mill."

When she did return to work, Crystal Lee knew one thing for certain: it was a relief to get out of the house again, even if only to work in a cotton mill.

On her first day back in the gift-sets section, Crystal Lee saw a new poster on the company bulletin board. It was a union notice advertising a meeting of the Textile Workers Union of America, to be held that coming Sunday in a small black church on the southern outskirts of Roanoke Rapids. The poster brought to her mind a letter she had received while off work.

The roots of that letter, which was from J. P. Stevens, went back to ten years earlier, 1963, when the TWUA began a campaign to organize mill hands at half of Stevens' seventy-five mills in the Carolinas. Stevens fought that campaign, in Roanoke Rapids and elsewhere, with brutal effectiveness—so brutal, in fact, that dozens of charges were brought against JP by the union in federal courts in the South, where the mills were, and in New York, where Stevens' headquarters were. In the fall of 1973, one of those cases, more than six years in litigation at that point, was settled by the U.S. Court of Appeals for the Second Circuit, in New York.

J. P. Stevens & Co., Inc., was found in civil contempt of two orders the court had issued six years earlier. Six of JP's bossmen, by name, also were found in civil contempt, and two of them, Mason Lee and Tommy Gardner, were among Crystal Lee's bossmen in the fab plant. The court ordered back pay amounting to tens of thousands of dollars each to men and women JP had fired for joining the union—not an unusual award, but the court also ordered Stevens to make a humiliating apology to all its mill hands. This apology had to be mailed, at company expense, to the home of every mill hand JP employed or had employed in the past six years. It had to be posted on every bulletin board in every Stevens mill. Further, Stevens had to assemble its hands on every shift and in every department, on company time, and let an agent of the National Labor Relations Board read to the mill hands the apology from the company. Not even that was the end. The court dictated, word for word, exactly what the apology had to say:

> The court has found that despite its two judgments we have discharged nine employes for engaging in union activities and one employe because he gave an affidavit to board investigators and was named as a board witness; and done acts forbidden by the court.
>
> We are now telling you sincerely that WE WILL NOT
>
> Encourage or discourage membership in the Textile Workers or any other union or take reprisal against anyone for giving testimony under the National Labor Relations Act:
>
> By discharging or forcing the termination of employes;
>
> By restricting the movements of employes within the plant;
>
> By downgrading the work of employes;
>
> By harassing employes;
>
> By making onerous work assignments to employes;

By changing the working conditions of employes;

By giving employes written or oral reprimands or write-ups or unfavorable personnel reports.

We also inform our employes that WE WILL NOT

Interrogate employes with respect to their or any other employes' Union activities;

Solicit reports about employees' Union activities;

Encourage employes to withdraw from the Union;

Threaten employes with discharge or other reprisal for engaging in Union activities;

Shadow employes in the plant or elsewhere for the purpose of spying on the Union activities;

Make inquiry or require any employes to inform supervisors as to the Union activity of employes.

There never had been anything like it in the history of the cotton mills, nor in the history of organized labor. But whether the court order would lead to union victories was another question. Textiles was the only basic industry in the nation that was not unionized; only 10 percent of the 700,000 Southern mill hands belonged to the TWUA. The union's campaign against Stevens, begun in 1963, had by 1973 won an election at only one plant. It was not that the mill hands did not want to join the union, but that Stevens intimidated them from doing so. That was the reason the union gave, and in part at least the union was right.

Crystal Lee had not thought about the union in years. When she and the other 3,700 mill hands in Roanoke Rapids got the JP apology in the mail she began to wonder what a union might change in the mills, and in her life. "It got me thinking about my parents, about me. You know, cotton-mill workers are known as trash by some, and I knew this union was the only way we could have our own voice, make ourselves better," she says.

Crystal Lee told Cookie about the union-meeting

notice she had seen on the bulletin board. "She asked me did I think it would be all right. The location of it was out in the country, in a black church. There wouldn't be many white people there. I told her I was sure nobody wouldn't bother her out there. And hell, I knew she would go anyway. I didn't much object to her going to the meeting. The only objection I had was the place it was taking place at. I said, 'Now you going on out there to a black church, out of town. You read about things happening to young women, and it could happen to you.' I just cautioned her about it, about things like that. But she don't believe nobody will bother her in that fashion. She just don't believe it. I've told her a thousand times that she's wrong feeling that way," Cookie says. Finally he told her, "All right, honey, but I'm telling you now you're going to get fired."

Cookie's answer was a precise illustration of what he had become in the marriage, what he had become both to Crystal Lee and to himself. She did not tell Cookie about the union meeting to ask his permission to go, or to solicit his assessment of what her going might bring either in threats at the meeting itself, or in retribution from JP for attending. No man who had not faced down Albert Pulley, not even when she asked him to, no man who when compared with her father seemed less a man than he, would ever command Crystal Lee's attention or respect. Even when she had laid bare the facts of her long affair with Ira Stonehouse, Cookie took it, seemed to accept it, not stoically, but meekly. Albert Pulley surely would have beaten her, and then Stonehouse, perhaps killed them both. But would a woman married to Albert Pulley ever seek another man in the first place? Crystal Lee did not think so.

Cookie Jordan suspected his wife thought these things about him. That she did, and even that he was forced by life to endure the situations and the men themselves, was to Cookie just more proof of what he had suspected since childhood: luck would never be with him. He believed every day held the strong chance that something bad was coming his way, and if something bad did not happen one day, it probably would the next, or the next, so that he was almost relieved when something bad finally did happen and he could say to himself he knew it would. This way, he had found, the bad things in his life were not so surprising to him. What would have surprised Cookie Jordan would be his telling Crystal Lee not to go to the union meeting, and her not going.

The meeting was at three-thirty Sunday afternoon in the Chockoyotte Baptist Church. Crystal Lee took the family car and picked up a friend, another white woman from the fabricating plant, on the way. When they drove up to the small red-brick church, they saw scores of cars parked in front. The chapel had been there since 1925, in a small black neighborhood of well-kept wood-frame houses. Crystal Lee had seen the church from the highway as a child, and knew the neighborhood was there, but she had never been to either. She did not know if black churches were the same as the churches she had been to. She knew that no church she had attended would open its doors to a union rally, much less a textile-union rally.

The day was bright and the spring weather mild outside, but when she and her friend walked inside the chapel, Crystal Lee could barely see to the altar. There were few lights inside, and the painted windows were only slightly open, letting in little light and less fresh air. The pews in front of her were full, she saw, and as her eyes grew accustomed to the dim light she also saw that every person in those pews was black. That a textile-union rally in a black church in Roanoke Rapids might attract only black mill hands had not occurred to her. She knew some of the blacks in the mills, but only a few, and those few she did not know well. There were nearly seventy black mill hands in the church. They seemed to take every seat, and Crystal Lee was about to find a spot to stand in the back when she saw an empty pew in front. She pointed it out to her friend and led the way down the aisle, taking a seat directly under the pulpit. Crystal Lee saw then that there were two more whites in the church, a man standing at the pulpit, and the woman he was talking with. They must be the union leaders, she assumed, and if so, she told herself, there was no doubt that it was the man who was in charge.

He was an older man, in his forties or early fifties, Crystal Lee thought. He was not big, although he struck her as strong, probably physically and emotionally strong, one of those men who look as though they always seem to know what to do next. The meeting had not yet started, and Crystal Lee found herself staring openly at the union man, catching herself looking at him when he glanced down at her. She did not turn away when the man looked at her, and when he smiled, she returned the smile.

By the time she got home from the rally that evening, she had decided to follow the man and his campaign. Cookie was full of questions—who was there, how many, had she had trouble, what was it like? Crystal Lee hardly spoke of anything from the rally other than the union man. Cookie remembered that later: "She was telling me of the things he had said. She was just impressed with the manner that he put himself across in. He had a way all his own. She said she'd never run across a man like that that felt the way that he did. And Eli really did. He's got a feeling for people, he really has. And she sensed that."

Eli Zivkovich, the man who so impressed Crystal Lee Jordan that Sunday afternoon in April, was unimpressive at first glance. He was relatively small, five feet ten, 155 pounds, and he was fifty-five years old then. But a closer look revealed a wiry, powerful man, his chest like a nail keg, with thick wrists and strong fingers. His straight black hair, streaked with gray, and his tanned, creased face gave an appearance not of a man of age but of a man of long experience, calmly powerful, a man who has earned his living at some time in his past by his own strength.

Two months before the union rally in Chockoyotte Baptist, Zivkovich had lost his job. He was an organizer in the West Virginia coal fields for the United Mine Workers. After twenty years in the fields for the UMW, Zivkovich and the union's new leaders clashed in a power struggle for the top offices. Eli backed the losing slate in elections. Before he was a union organizer he had been a coal miner, as his father and grandfather had been. When the UMW fired him, Eli had a daughter still in high school, and one of his two sons was still in college. His wife, Pearl, a registered nurse, was supporting the family on her income alone. Eli spent several weeks in a fruitless search for work with other unions, and during that time heard that the textile union needed organizers in the Stevens campaign. He had not applied for those jobs because he knew nothing about textiles. One day in late March, as Eli sat in the office of a Steelworkers Union friend in Pittsburgh, the phone rang. The caller was Paul Swaity, the chief of organizing for the textile union. Swaity told Eli's friend that he needed a good organizer, and the friend said, "I'm looking at a guy right now who will fill your bill." Eli took the job over the phone. "My heart lies with the miners, but I didn't want to leave the labor movement," he said later.

While he did not know the inside of a cotton mill, Eli did know life in company towns. "I grew up in the Henry Clay Frick domain. Frick produced coal for Andrew Carnegie's steel mills. They were captive mines owned by the steel companies. Back then they had the Coal and Iron Police, state cops they hired and the mines and steel mills paid—Frick and Carnegie. We called them 'yellow dogs' because they wore yellow uniforms. They'd come right up and break up a conversation between neighbors, do anything," Eli says.

His salary dropped from $15,000 a year with the UMW to $9,000 a year with the TWUA, and the job, in the South, would keep him from home. But Eli accepted the offer, and before he hung up the phone his new boss had told him to report to the union office in Charlotte, North Carolina, on a Monday, April 9. At nine o'clock on that morning, Eli walked into the office. It took him less than an hour to complete his employment papers, and by ten o'clock he was on the road.

"The only thing I knew then about textiles was that the Stevens campaign had been going on unsuccessfully for years. The thing that I could never understand was the fact that here was a basic industry that hasn't really been touched. This does not make sense to me to this day. The way of life, this paternalistic system of life, maybe just did not allow for any successes, because the people are different down here," Eli says.

But he did think it was possible to beat the mill owners, just as his old union beat Carnegie, Frick and the other mine owners.

Eli spent that first week in Greenville, South Carolina, and in small mill towns near there. He handed out TWUA leaflets to mill hands during shift changes at Stevens' plants. It was the first time he had seen a textile mill, and the first time he had seen cotton-mill hands, and the sight surprised him. "When we organized in the mines, we didn't have large units. A large coal-mine operation would be like a fifty-man operation. You developed a personal contact. You lived with the people. Here in the South, the first plant I leafed was Dunean, outside Greenville. Good God, it was like twenty-five hundred workers," Eli remembered.

The leafleting at Stevens mills near Greenville was part of the same union leaflet drive that had taken place two weeks earlier at the Stevens mills in Roanoke Rapids. Both efforts were part of a search by the textile union to find at least one Stevens town where the workers might respond to the company apology being read in the Stevens mills then. Each leaflet had a postcard in it that could be mailed to the union office in Charlotte if the worker wanted to know more about the TWUA. The union hoped for response from some mill, some town, but no one in the union expected the response that came in the mail from Roanoke Rapids. There had not been a TWUA meeting in Roanoke Rapids in eight years. When 350 postcards came in from Roanoke Rapids, almost 10 percent of the entire work force responding to the single leaflet, the union was surprised, and at a loss to explain what might be happening in Roanoke Rapids to account for that.

"I came back to Charlotte, checked in a motel, and first thing I know we're headed up to Roanoke Rapids," Eli said. That was a Sunday, April 15, 1973, six days after Eli had gone to work for the TWUA.

He put his suitcases in his own car, a blue four-door sedan he had driven from home in Fairmont, West Virginia. Ahead of Eli in another car on the road to Roanoke Rapids were two more union men: Harold McIver, Eli's immediate supervisor and chief of the North Carolina organizing activities for the Industrial Union Department of the AFL-CIO, and Mel Tate, an organizer from Georgia hired for the Stevens campaign the same week Eli was. "I got my first Southern barbecue on the way, pork, at some little town. And then we drove into Roanoke Rapids, to the paperworkers' union hall on the main street. It was locked. We waited around until someone came to unlock the hall," Eli says.

Word of the meeting had spread casually in Roanoke Rapids that week after one mill hand in the town —no one remembers who—telephoned the Charlotte union office and asked for organizers. More than a hundred mill hands were at the union hall. Neither McIver nor anyone else in the union had a strategy to give them, or to give to Eli Zivkovich. It had been so long since the textile union had tried to launch a major campaign, one that brought several organizers at once into contact with hundreds of mill hands, that no one in the union's ranks had recent experience to draw on.

Eli explained what happened. "I didn't know anything about Roanoke Rapids. I didn't know where I was going, except that I was going to a meeting of some more textile workers. I didn't really know that I was gonna be stationed there until we had the meeting, and it was Harold's thinking that this place should be taken on again. I don't know that Harold even knew before he got there. It was all going to be based on response," he says. McIver opened the meeting. As he spoke, Eli learned what his new job was. McIver turned to him, in front of the crowd, and said Eli was their new organizer. He would be staying in Roanoke Rapids indefinitely, McIver said. He asked Eli to say a few words then. "I just told them that I, you know, I'm pleased to be here with you; we're gonna make this thing move, and it's gonna start here. I remember vividly making that statement: that it'll all start here in Roanoke Rapids," Eli says now. Every worker in the hall, except one, was black. And black or white, Eli could not catch what they said. "I just couldn't understand the Southern worker's accent when I first came, and I had to read their lips," he says.

The union was as new to the workers in that hall as the cotton mills and this haphazard way of starting a major campaign were to Eli. When the meeting ended, McIver took Eli to his new office, a motel room fifty yards from the chain-link fences surrounding the biggest Stevens mill in town. Eli had a small room, number seven, hardly fifteen feet square, and crowded with a bed, two desks and three chairs. The motel, the Motel Dixie, was an old two-story brick building. It was built in a block C, with all the rooms opening onto a small blacktop parking lot. In the middle of the parking lot was a small swimming pool. Eli looked out from his doorway and saw beer cans and scraps of paper floating in the water. The motel was one block west of Roanoke Avenue, the main street, and one block east of Rosemary mill, at the southern end of downtown, not far from the old Junction neighborhood where Cookie Jordan had spent part of his childhood.

Most of the motel's patrons were struggling traveling salesmen and the most budget-minded tourists who picked Motel Dixie for its cheap rates. "McIver said this would be it, go get 'em, organize. And they would probably send me help," Eli says. By sunset he was alone in the room, wondering how he would start the campaign, not knowing anyone in town. He did not have long to wait.

There was a knock on the door. When Eli opened it he saw two white men standing there, neither of them from the afternoon meeting. They did not speak at first, and then almost in unison each stuck out a hand. Both of them had small blue cards, which Eli recognized as TWUA membership cards. The two men were the first mill hands in Roanoke Rapids to join his campaign. "I told them, 'Good God, keep them rolling.' Well, within the next two or three days Joseph Williams, a black man who attended that first meeting with his brother and his dad, came in. And I think Joe brought me fifty or sixty cards. Another guy came in with forty cards, and these guys was hanging real close. I thought, good God, this thing's going to happen overnight here," Eli says.

McIver had taken no chance in the Sunday meeting that any mill hand in the hall might have missed a copy of the court order and the Stevens apology. He read all of it and emphasized that the order meant the mill hands could wear TWUA buttons on their shirts when they went to work, and could talk about the union to any other mill hand who wanted to listen, in the plant during breaks, as long as it did not stop anyone from working. They could take union pamphlets to the mills, and pass those along, he had said, and in all of that, there was nothing the company could do to them because the court could throw a bossman in jail or fine him. McIver urged the mill hands to recruit union members from inside the six mills, and the men and women at the meeting began to do so.

On April 18, the Wednesday after that first meeting, Stevens struck back. Three white supervisors in Delta #4 cornered a black worker who was handing out leaflets on the work floor during a ten-minute break. The bossmen told him he would be fired unless he confined his leafleting to the company canteen. That same day Stevens began a new policy: a supervisor stood against the wall inside every canteen for the duration of the two ten-minute breaks and the twenty-minute lunch period each shift had.

And on that Wednesday, in the Patterson mill, the plant superintendent cornered another black mill hand, asked him if he supported the union, asked him who his fellow leaflet distributor was, and ordered him not to pass out leaflets on company property. The other leafleter, Joseph Williams, who had taken new membership cards to Eli's motel room the night before, was told by the bossmen to put up his leaflets or be fired.

Crystal Lee Jordan knew nothing of these skirmishes when she returned to work in the fabricating plant in late April. Few mill hands in town knew it when the company fired Joseph Williams in mid-May, or when JP fired a woman talking for the union in the canteen. Most of the union sympathizers were black, and they did not talk freely with the white mill hands about the campaign or the firings. The textile union was far too controversial, and the silent suspicion between whites and blacks far too ingrained, to allow open talk of the union between the races. Eli knew of each firing, each harassment, because the workers came by his motel room at the end of the shifts that week and told him. He wrote down the details, took names of witnesses, typed long reports, and added it all to the list he hoped the union would take to court eventually.

But more legal maneuvers were not going to be enough to launch a major campaign, Eli thought. He needed a dramatic move, not only to let the company know he meant business, but to let the mill hands know that whatever might have happened in old TWUA campaigns, he, Eli Zivkovich, who had spent twenty years working for the union in the coal fields, was not about to be pushed around by some cotton-mill bossmen. He found his tactic on Thursday, the day after JP's resistance began, when he noticed a short clause in the federal court order. It said the union had the right to inspect every bulletin board in the mills at least once a week. The union could verify, in person, that its notices were not being stripped from the boards. No union organizer, not even a known union member, had been inside the fences and walls of any J. P. Stevens cotton mill in more than a decade. No one in Roanoke Rapids, Eli learned then, not the company supervisors themselves, remembered the last time a union organizer even tried to get inside. Eli walked in that day.

He drove to the office of the man who supervised all JP's mills in town. "I met his assistant, a fellow who had steel in his eye, and I walked in, and he didn't expect this kind of thing. I walked in and introduced myself like I was a cousin. I let him know I'm here, brother, and I want to look at your plants. I didn't even know where all the plants in Roanoke Rapids were. Well, I could tell, looking at the son of a gun, he was angry. He left the room and was gone for a period of time, and I knew what the hell he was doing. He was consulting with his bosses. Well, he come back, had a guide for me, and I got in the guide's car, and he took me to each of the plants, introduced me to each plant manager. I went to every bulletin board. They usually give you ear plugs to wear inside, because of the noise, but they didn't give me any, and I couldn't understand because there again I'm a Northerner listening to some of these Southerners, and I'm telling you it was hard reading lips where there was that noise," Eli says.

Had she been back at work then, Crystal Lee might have seen Eli that day. She would have been as startled at the sight of a union man inside the mills as were the workers who saw Eli and recognized what he was. The first mill he went to was Rosemary. One of the bossmen waiting for Eli at the gate was Tommy Gardner, who had been cited by name in the court order forbidding further harassment of mill hands. "I asked him if he was the man that was named in the contempt citation, and he didn't answer me," Eli says. "They did it real Gestapo-fashion. What they did is the superintendent was ahead of me. I was behind him, and the guide behind me. Like when you're in a prison and you have someone in front of you, someone behind you. Now, by the time I got to the second mill, that didn't make me feel good, so what I did, I just stepped back to where we were either together, or I was behind them. I had my pad and my pencil, and I'd stop and speak to the workers. Not that many workers, but I was the one who was doing some impressing. There was a lot of bulletin-board space in there, and what those fuckers would do, they'd have a cloth there so it'd be inconvenient for anyone to see the bulletin board. I fussed with them right on the spot, about putting the thing out there at eye level where it could be read by the workers. They said that they would take note, and I said, 'Well, I'll check with our lawyers and find out how much note-taking you're going to do, because the damn thing ought to be available now and not waste a day or two checking on it.' I was heading for the phone right then," Eli says.

When he got to the Patterson mill, the third of the six he toured that day, the company had its own strategy for handling Eli's surprise inspection. One of JP's toughest bossmen waited for him, met him at the first Patterson bulletin board. When Eli began reading what was on the board, the man stepped up and said, "You're not supposed to read the damned thing."

Eli, who described that bossman as one who "wears his JP button not only on the lapel, but on the soul," pivoted around and faced the man. "Brother, I only want to see if it's all here," Eli said.

"It's there. Now keep moving," the bossman said.

"Now, brother, I didn't know whether you read that court order or not, or remember it says not only those named specifically, but any agent of the company can be held in contempt. Now you're messing with a contempt citation, and if you want to go to jail, just keep it up," Eli said.

"I don't violate no laws," the bossman said, and Eli told him, "Well, baby, you're violating a law now."

Another bossman met Eli at the gate of the next mill. "He refused to shake my hand, handed me some damn earmuffs, and wheeled on his heels and took off like a striped ape," Eli says. Eli watched him go, fifty feet, then a hundred, until the bossman realized Eli was not in step behind him. When the man came back to the gate, Eli told him, "Look, man, I don't do high port. I did my running when I was in the Marine Corps. I'm not in the Marine Corps now." The two men almost strolled through that mill, Eli says. "The longer I was in the plant, the more exposure, and the more irritating it would be to them," he said. "What I would do then, I would look at the bulletin board, hell, it only takes you a minute to see everything's in order, then I'd face the workers in the other direction. And what he would do, he was tall, much taller than me, he'd block my view. So we developed a two-step. I'd go like this and wait, and he'd get in front of me, and I'd come back over here and wait." The bossman grew angrier after each stop by a bulletin board. He said nothing about it to Eli, and the two men soon were joined by two other men, both bossmen, both of them taller and broader than Eli. The next board was in a warehouse, and fewer than a dozen mill hands worked in the long building.

No one else was in sight as the four men approached the board. There were boxes and bolts of cloth in front of it, completely blocking the board, and the sight angered Eli. "Move it. Move it now," he said. "You're in trouble, man, you know you can go to jail for this," he told the supervisor. The three bossmen formed a semicircle behind Eli. He backed to the bulletin board. Then five black mill hands walked out between the rows of boxes. They stopped and looked. No one spoke for a moment. The supervisor looked at the five black men, then at his two assistants, and he said to the two, "Move the stuff."

The inspection tour not only made Eli visible in the cotton mills, but it also gave him the details he needed to let the mill hands know that he realized what life was like inside the brick walls of JP's six mills in Roanoke Rapids. Eli called another meeting in the paperworkers' hall the next Sunday. He gave his first long speech then, and he remembered it later. "I told them how closely related I am to the cotton-mill worker. I ate the dust in the coal mine. I says, 'I can't even see your dust, but I feel it. I've got to wash, and

I sneeze. My eyes run when I have to go through your plants. Now you're in there eight hours a day. We're going to have to do something about that. We're going to have to organize.' Well, that style of showing that I am not a stranger, if anything, perhaps more related to a cotton mill worker than any other basic industry worker, it helped," Eli says. There was more to his speech. " 'The dust, the noise, the artificial light you have to work under.' I told them that we're going to have to tear that fence down from the mills, going to have to push those windows back out. I told them, 'The company says they brick up the windows for air conditioning. What the hell? Who's kidding who? The company bricked up those windows to give the workers that feeling that they're shut in, and we control your soul, brother or sister, for all this period, and beware.' And I told them that we were going to meet, and we were going to feed JP union until it pours out of their ears. Every time I see a new face in a meeting, well, that person has to be told. That is the secret to any campaign. It's not the organizer that does it. It's the worker in the plant that does it," Eli says.

This was the speech Crystal Lee heard at her first union meeting. And when Eli saw her, another new face, he caught her eye and spoke directly to her. She thought at the time that this man was talking to no one else in the church, almost as though no one were there except Eli and Crystal Lee.

Eli wanted Crystal Lee in his campaign the moment he saw her, wanted her then simply because she was white, unlike nearly all the other mill hands in the union ranks. Eli alone could never organize a fraction of the 3,700 workers in JP's six mills. Left alone in town with nothing more than a motel room and a word of encouragement, he had no one to turn to but the workers themselves. He did not know what the union had done in Roanoke Rapids before. He did ask McIver to mail the background on the town and the union, but McIver never did. Nor did anyone in the union tell Eli about three women in Roanoke Rapids, former mill hands awarded almost $30,000 each in back pay and interest by the federal court. He could have used them, he once said, as living examples of how Stevens could be whipped. There was a reason for that omission, and Eli found out about it months later, from Crystal Lee Jordan. When the three women were fired by Stevens for their union activity, the TWUA took their cases to court, but that was all the union did. The campaign faded away, and the women spent years on the cotton-mill blacklist, unable to find work at any non-union mill. "There must have been a long time between meals for them, and I can't blame them for being bitter at the union," Eli said.

Eli's first weekly organizer's report, mailed to his bosses in Charlotte, said, "Major problem is lack of white interest. Objective is to organize a committee of in-plant workers who can organize, and to get to the white mill hand." Of the 3,700 workers JP had in town, less than 700 were black then. And while that was twice as many as five years before, it was far from the majority of card-signers the union needed to call for an election. The election itself, if and when it was held, would only determine whether or not a majority of the workers wanted the union to bargain for them. If the union won the election, there would still be weeks, perhaps months, of negotiations before a contract might be signed.

The union sent Eli an assistant during his second week in Roanoke Rapids, a former mill hand from a small plant in upstate New York who had no experience as a full-time organizer. She would be his only staff, Eli was told. The woman, Margaret Banks, left a purely physical first impression on Eli. She was enormous, her body a caricature of a fat lady. She wore black ballet slippers on tiny feet, which almost disappeared beneath the rest of her, and the pedal pushers and slacks she wore bulged from hip to knee with the bulk they held. Often she wore shirts and sweaters so luminous, so bright with oranges, pinks, pale greens and blues, that, what with her clothes and her bright-orange hair, she seemed to have dressed herself in spray paint. She rarely spoke, rarely moved once seated, and almost never made any small gesture, a wave of her hand, a laugh. There was little else to gauge her by, except at times when you could spin around quickly in the same room with Margaret Banks and find her peering at you.

The two of them, Eli and Margaret, went to work, shrugging off fear of reprisals from Stevens. Eli never worried whether or not his phone was tapped or his room bugged by JP, but just assumed that both had happened. That coming winter, in Wallace, South Carolina, where the union had a similar campaign underway at other Stevens mills, taps were found on the motel phones of the union organizers. The Federal Bureau of Investigation traced the taps to two JP supervisors who eventually were tried and convicted for the spying.

Eli found a constant fear of JP, and suspicion of whites, among the black workers he met in the first weeks of the campaign. "My motel door would be open under cover of darkness, or we'd set up a small meeting, five or six at a time, in someone's house," he said. But despite the fear of JP's reprisals, the black mill hands filled the paperworkers' hall so tightly that by the end of April Eli was looking for a larger meeting hall. He was offered a church—Chockoyotte Baptist Church—by one of the black workers, and he saw no reason not to hold his next Sunday rally in it. That was the union rally Crystal Lee Jordan attended.

"There was two white girls right in the front row, and I says, 'Good Lord, Margaret, things are happening,' because it was our first real white response, small as it was, and we had to get to those people," Eli recalls. He sought out Crystal Lee when the rally ended. "Crystal told me then she didn't know anything about the union. I told Margaret to get the phone numbers, hers and the other woman, and I called her the next day and asked her to come by the office. I wanted to talk with her and explain to her that it's imperative we get the white people involved here. I said to her, 'For God's sakes, show up at the meetings and bring your white friends.' She didn't, though, not the first few times. She'd show up at the meetings and take notes, and people didn't know her. I didn't know her. Margaret thought right off she was a company spy, and I didn't know what to think. She hadn't signed a membership card or anything in writing. But I did see interest in her eyes," Eli says.

Crystal Lee was a suspect in the minds of the black workers, in Eli's mind, in Margaret's, but she did not realize it. Cookie thought she would be suspected. "I had the feeling these black people were saying she is a spy for the company," he says. But Cookie did not mention that to Crystal Lee. She might have laughed at him if he had. He had never before seen Crystal Lee as excited as she was after her first union rally, excited about the union and the union man. This did not make him jealous, however, because at the time, Cookie supposed Crystal Lee looked at the union, and at Eli, in the way she might look at a new church and a new preacher. If she liked it, that was fine with him. It might take her mind off her problems, he thought. She even acted like a reformed sinner.

"I was really ready to go," Crystal Lee says. "Man, I got me the biggest TWUA button Eli had, and wore it to work the next day." An hour after she walked in the gate wearing that five-inch-wide badge that proclaimed in red letters on white "I'm for TWUA," she was in trouble. A foreman, Eugene Taylor, wanted to know why she was wearing a union button. "I told him it was none of his damn business," Crystal Lee said. She told him with a smile on her face, and she was surprised at herself for saying it at all. "I don't know why, but it made me feel good to say that. It was like it didn't make any difference what Eugene Taylor did about it, or what JP did," she says. "I didn't want to lose my job. But it was funny, like it didn't make any difference if I did or not, and I didn't know why it didn't make any difference. But it didn't," she says.

Crystal Lee had been bored and listless at work, and now the real danger of being fired for talking up the union replaced that boredom and made her eager to get to the mill each day. She brought the union into her home, too, offering the house for use as a union conference spot. "She lives between two supervisors for JP, and she told me that," Eli says. "You might have thought she was setting us up, getting us to bring our people by her house so JP could see who we had on our side then, so those supervisors could look out the window and see. But I figured they were already taking down license numbers wherever we were, and I wanted to let JP know I wasn't afraid of that, or of them, and let the workers know they didn't have to be either," he says.

Crystal Lee got an organizer's card from Eli. "I started in the canteens, on the break time," she says. "I would talk union to my friends, and I started getting a lot of membership cards signed." She brought white mill hands by the Motel Dixie before her shift started at four in the afternoons, and after it ended at midnight. She told Eli early in May that if JP was spying on the union, she was going to spy right back on JP. The company ordered its workers to answer an "opinion survey" that had a question in it Crystal Lee suspected was anti-union. "Do you think a union would help or hurt the employes of this company?" it asked, and the questionnaire had to be signed by each worker. Crystal Lee slipped a copy out of the mill and gave it to Eli. She saw him at the motel at least twice a day in early May. On her days off, she brought Mark, Jay and Elizabeth with her and joined Margaret Banks in keeping the union paperwork up to date. She did every small chore Eli asked of her, and suggested others when he had nothing specific for her to do.

And when he realized what she was doing, Cookie began to warn Crystal Lee. "When she got into this thing, when she started campaigning for the union, I said, 'Sister, you're going to get fired.' Every day I carried her up to work, I said this is liable to be her last day. But I had no objections to her being a union member. I didn't want her to get into it the way she did. I mean, I just didn't want her to be a front-runner. I didn't want that. But that's the way it happened," Cookie says.

Cookie had not met Eli nor any of the mill hands in the campaign. When Crystal Lee volunteered their home for union meetings, Cookie avoided her new friends and missed the meetings by leaving the house, going fishing or out with his friends until he knew the meeting was over. He was nervous—not just out of fear of Crystal Lee's losing her job, but also out of fear of what his neighbors might say about all the blacks, a rare sight in their all-white neighborhood, going in and out of his house.

"I've often thought of how it made my wife feel with three or four supervisors of JP living right there, seeing everything going on at our house, and seeing twelve or fifteen cars parked at our house, and folks parked in the street, in the drive. And seeing black people standing in the front yard and all, sitting around talking, and knowing that they were sitting around talking. I often wondered how it made my wife feel. But it never made her fearful, although I had told her to accept the fact: the least little thing she did wrong, they were going to get rid of her. She knew it, but it really hadn't sunk in. She didn't really believe that they would get rid of her for doing what she did," Cookie says.

By the end of May, no other union sympathizer in town, no one Eli had seen in twenty years of union work, seemed to have the zeal Crystal Lee had. And if her enthusiasm for the campaign came from her restlessness at work and at home, which Eli suspected it might, if this campaign was for her a chance to escape that routine, then that was fine with Eli. He took her up on her every offer, for thirty days in May, until on the night of May 30, Eli gave Crystal Lee the last union mission she would have inside the walls of a cotton mill.

5

MEMORIAL DAY is not much of a holiday in the South. Hardly anyone other than federal office workers takes a day off for it. In 1973, Memorial Day fell on a Wednesday—May 30—and in Roanoke Rapids, the cotton mills owned by J. P. Stevens ran full shifts that day; few of the mill hands would have thought the day unusual except, perhaps, for the presence of the portable radios many of them brought to work to listen to the stock-car race in Darlington, South Carolina.

Eli Zivkovich began the day with a problem.

The week before, he had heard of a four-page letter JP had posted on some of the bulletin boards in the six mills. Eli did not see the letter when he made his bulletin-board inspection tour, but some of the black mill hands told him about parts of it. They said it had the usual anti-union messages, and it also had something new, a carefully worded section about black mill hands and the union. None of them could say exactly what that section or the full letter said because the bossmen, the mill hands told Eli, were keeping watch on the bulletin boards so no one could copy the letter. "I wanted that information, because I felt that anything like that our office in Charlotte should know about right now, so they could get out an answer to it, and if there's any legal action, it can be taken," Eli says. He was not certain that week whether he would have time to make his usual inspection tour.

Two days before Memorial Day, on Monday, Eli had asked one of the women in the fabricating plant either to get a copy of the letter or to copy it herself when the bossmen were not looking. But the foremen had watched the bulletin boards too closely. On Tuesday, Crystal Lee heard what the other woman had tried. She decided to copy the letter herself and surprise Eli with it. But when she tried to, the assistant overseer of the plant, Dave Moody, walked up to Crystal Lee by the bulletin board and told her no one was allowed to make copies of that letter.

While Crystal Lee was trying to copy the letter for Eli, Eli was reaching a decision about Crystal Lee. He was nearly ready to accept her without suspicion. "She appeared to be fearless to me. She appeared to be intelligent, and she appeared sincere. She impressed me as one who if she said she was going to do something she'd do it. And when the other woman couldn't get the letter, well, what I really felt was, here is a test, for Crystal," Eli says. On Memorial Day afternoon Eli called Crystal Lee and asked her to come by the motel before her shift started at four. He explained to her how badly he wanted a copy of the letter, and said she was the only one left who could get it.

By late afternoon, when Cookie drove Crystal Lee to work, the temperature was approaching 90 and the humidity was nearly as high. There are no shade trees within a block of the fabricating plant, and the air was so still and heavy with humidity that Crystal Lee took in as little of it as possible, breathing in short sucks as she walked through the gate in the chain-link fence and opened the door to the mill. It was three thirty-five when she walked through the doorway, and she was twenty-five minutes early for work.

Crystal Lee wanted it that way. She planned to sip coffee in the canteen off the shearing-room floor and talk union with one or two mill hands. There are two canteens off the main floor, a new one and an old one. They are the only authorized places for mill hands to take their ten-minute breaks or twenty-minute meals, and for more than a month, since the union campaign had begun, JP had kept a bossman in each one at all times. The canteens are long, narrow rooms, brightly lit by fluorescent bulbs. Although each one holds coin vending machines for coffee, soft drinks, ice cream, milk, crackers, candy and sandwiches, as well as five plastic tables with plastic chairs, they manage to appear empty and barren, not at all the kind of spot to tempt a mill hand to stay awhile longer and talk.

Crystal Lee went to the old canteen, bought a pack of potato chips and a cup of coffee, which she cooled with ice water from the water fountain, and then sat with two other mill hands waiting for the second shift to begin. A bossman she did not recognize, probably one from another section of the plant, stood by the canteen door. Crystal Lee smiled at the bossman; then, without lowering her voice, she said to one of the workers sitting with her, "You ought to join up in the union with me." He grinned at her, ducked his head, and said, a little quietly, "Sure, and I ought to get fired and go on welfare too." Crystal Lee did not hard-sell the union in these canteen talks. She did not press the issue then, but lowered her voice and joined the other two in casual talk, not mentioning the union again. She finished her coffee, saw the time on the wall clock, then left the canteen and walked to her folding table on the floor. Melvia Reed, Crystal Lee's forelady and immediate supervisor, was waiting for her.

"Ray Mabry wants you in the office," Melvia Reed said. Mabry was one of the fabricating-plant bossmen, called the overseer. His air-conditioned office was twenty yards behind Crystal Lee's folding table. Glass partitions divided Mabry's office, and those of other bossmen, from the open floor of the shearing room. The bossmen can see at a glance through their windows every corner of the huge floor. When Crystal Lee walked into Mabry's office, she remembered later, she had her chin up and a smile set on her face. She felt good, very good. Being sent to Mabry's office probably meant trouble, she thought then, but she still felt good. She had had that feeling from the time she had left Eli's motel room with his instructions to copy the letter. That was going to lead to trouble, she expected, and she had no idea yet how she would copy the letter without getting caught. Something would occur to her, she thought.

"Man, is it cool in here," Crystal Lee told Mabry when she walked into his office, "Boy, it really feels good." Without waiting to be asked, Crystal Lee sat down across the desk from the overseer. Mabry had no small talk to give her. "Lee, why did you go to the old canteen? Haven't you been instructed to eat in the new canteen?" he asked. Crystal Lee was surprised that all Mabry wanted to talk about was whether or not she used one canteen or another. There was more to this than that, she told herself, but she answered Mabry's question: "No, sir, Ray. Melvia came around Monday and said our break time was changed. But she didn't say, 'Y'all have to eat in the new canteen.' Besides, Ray, I like to cool my coffee down, and there's no water fountain in the new canteen, so I'd have to carry that hot coffee all across the floor to the old canteen to cool it down. And the new canteen, it doesn't have a potato-chip machine, and I like potato chips with my coffee."

"Well, I didn't know that you had not been instructed," Mabry told her. "I'll tell everyone where they're supposed to go on breaks," he said, and after a moment's pause, while he looked at her steadily, Mabry asked Crystal Lee, "Is there anything else you'd like to talk about?" Was this an invitation to talk about the union, she wondered, or about Dave Moody, Mabry's assistant, chasing her away from the bulletin board the night before? If it were, Crystal Lee decided, she was not going to take up the offer. She had another complaint to make. "Yes, Ray, I'd like to talk about the fence, about the gate being locked."

The chain-link fences, some with barbed-wire strands on top, that surround the six Stevens cotton mills in town are broached only by turnstiles and gates. Each gate has a bell button, and at night the gates are locked, making it impossible for anyone to enter or leave without a bossman unlocking the gate. The Friday before Memorial Day, a rainy night, the gate bell outside the fabricating-plant door rang for fifteen minutes before a bossman answered it. That time it was a new mill hand, a young girl reporting to work with a forelady. Another time, Crystal Lee told Mabry, at midnight when the second shift was leaving and the third shift coming on, the locked gate kept the two groups of mill hands from getting in or out for ten minutes until a supervisor arrived with the key.

"How many people around here have keys?" Crystal Lee asked Mabry now.

"Well, I have one, and Dave Moody, and I think James Alston"—Mabry's boss—"has one," he said.

"Well, that may be, but since I've been to work for the last month I've noticed these people are awfully slow getting to the gate when the bell rings, and people are saying, 'Well, maybe that's somebody for me. Maybe it's an emergency,'" Crystal Lee told him.

Mabry listened to Crystal Lee's complaint without speaking. When she finished, he did not ask her a second time if there was anything else. "I'll look into it. You can go back to work now," he told Crystal Lee.

She was almost giddy with excitement when she walked out of the bossman's office, Crystal Lee remembers, and it struck her then that this was an odd time to be feeling that. It was not as if she had actually defied her bossman and gotten away with it, because she had not. Something was on her mind, and something was making her feel unusually good tonight. She could feel herself reacting to it, feeling alert and quick, walking smartly back to her folding table, and smiling at the other women she passed on the way. Crystal Lee tried to puzzle it out then, absently folding more towels, and her thought wandered back to her childhood in Roanoke Rapids and Burlington. "My father really wanted me to get a high school education. If it hadn't been for my father, I would have quit. He always told me, 'If you don't get that high school education, you're going to end up in the cotton mills just like me.' Well, here I am with the high school education, and still I'm in the cotton mills. Maybe it's just in me. My parents were cotton-mill workers. I was never ashamed of the way that we lived. It is just a fact of living," Crystal Lee says now. And while she folded more towels that night, Crystal Lee wondered if she would always work in the cotton mills and live in a cotton-mill town.

Her life with Cookie came to mind too, their frustrating marriage, her affair, the affair with Jay's father, her short marriage to Junior Wood. "Wherever I am, there always has been a lot of men. Girls just don't like me. Maybe it's always been me," she thought. And it occurred to her then that the times she spent with Albert Pulley, Junior, Cookie, all of them, had one thing in common: "All my life it seems like I've been told what to do. Even when I was married to Cookie, I had Daddy as a boss. And I had Cookie as a boss. All my life I've always had to get permission from a man, and I'm tired of it." Even now, Eli was telling her what to do, making her promise to copy the new letter on the bulletin board tonight.

Crystal Lee waited until break time, close to six o'clock, and then waved to another woman working in gift sets and motioned for the woman to join her in the restroom. No one else was in the restroom—Crystal Lee checked each stall before she spoke—and she told the other woman her plan. The other woman was one of Crystal Lee's best friends in the mill, and although she had not signed a union card (she said she was afraid to), she had gone with Crystal Lee to her first union meeting, in the black church, and talked about the union enough to persuade Crystal Lee she could be trusted. It might take a few days to finish it, but this was the plan, Crystal Lee said. Each of them would memorize one paragraph at a time, then go to the restroom, write the fragment on scrap paper, hide the paper in their bras, and return to work. Perhaps they could copy a page each tonight, and get the rest tomorrow, Crystal Lee said.

The plan, or the chance to break the boredom of the shift in a harmless plot against JP, appealed to Crystal Lee's friend, and she agreed to help. The two women began giggling about it then. Crystal Lee felt so good about the way things seemed to be going that she did an elaborate pantomime of a secret agent skulking around the women's restroom. "You suppose this place is bugged?" she whispered to her friend. "Maybe they're listening to us right now," Crystal Lee suggested, and the thought of hidden microphones in the bathroom made them both laugh aloud. The other woman pulled a cigarette from her purse, lit it, which was against company rules in the restroom, then winked and asked Crystal Lee, "You suppose they can hear me doing this?" Crystal Lee tiptoed to the towel dispenser and whispered to it, "Can you hear me?" The other woman crept to the mirror and waved at it as though someone on the other side could see her. Crystal Lee walked to the trash can and leaned over it to say, "Hey, this is me." The two left the restroom in giggles.

But the plan was not good enough. For one thing, both women kept forgetting their lines in the walk from the bulletin board to the restroom. And then the other woman noticed Ray Mabry and Dave Moody, the overseers, watching her read the letter, and she told Crystal Lee she was afraid to copy any more. By eight o'clock the two had managed to copy one and a half paragraphs, and Crystal Lee had those notes hidden in her bra. It was going too slowly. Crystal Lee decided to phone Eli and tell him she would have to try another method the next day.

When she reached him at the Motel Dixie, Eli was finishing the day's paperwork and was in a hurry to leave.

"Eli, I need some more support here. I can't get the letter by myself," Crystal Lee began. "Now Crystal, you're gonna have to get that information off that bulletin board," Eli answered. The idea of testing her loyalty, her willingness to take chances for his campaign, occurred to Eli then. He remembers their conversation: "I said we need that letter, and she said, 'I'm hungry,' and I said, 'Get the thing, Crystal. Get it.' Crystal says, 'I haven't eaten yet,' and I says, 'Look, it ain't gonna take you all that long. Copy it and get it to me. Copy it and then go eat your supper.'" Crystal Lee said she would try again.

When Eli put down the phone he was confident Crystal Lee would present him with the letter the next day at the motel. The last thing Crystal Lee had told him on the phone was, "Eli, I'm going to copy down all of that letter tonight."

There was a "safety supper" that evening in the fabricating plant to mark the passage of one million man-hours at work without a lost-time accident by a mill hand. JP bought the food for such occasions, and tonight the menu was one of Crystal Lee's favorites: barbecued chicken, hushpuppies, barbecued potatoes, brunswick stew and iced tea from Ralph's Barbecue, the town's most popular restaurant. Crystal Lee watched as the women from gift sets, and the mill hands from the put-up department, and then the side hemmers and terry cutters walked off the shearing-room floor to the serving tables set up in a storage room nearby. She really was hungry, Crystal Lee told herself, and she was irritated over Eli's insistence that she get the letter copied tonight. She did not see anyone near her at her end of the long room, so she picked up a clipboard she kept at her folding table to list the gift sets she wrapped, and she walked straight to the bulletin board to copy the letter openly, but quickly, before the bossmen might return.

Crystal Lee read the first few paragraphs of the four-page letter. It was addressed "to all employees," and there was nothing on the first page that struck her as unusual. "If this union were to get in here, there is no way that it could force this company to do anything that we might not consider to be reasonable or practicable. It might try to force the company by pulling you out on strike. We hope you will understand, however, that this company has no intention of yielding to any sort of strike pressure at any time," the last paragraph of the first page said. Crystal Lee wrote that down. Nothing unusual there, she thought, just the usual JP line. She looked around the room behind her. Still no one else near her.

Crystal Lee went on to page two. "There is no denying the fact that where unions are is where strikes generally occur. Everyone knows that. And everybody knows that strikes mean loss of work, loss of pay and often loss of jobs—strain and strife and trouble and dissension, which frequently ends up in serious violence," the letter said. More of the usual JP line, Crystal Lee thought as she copied that passage down. Why is it so important Eli see this? she asked herself. She looked behind her again, but did not notice anyone near her, so she went on to page three. When she got to the fifth paragraph on that page, Crystal Lee began scribbling faster on her clipboard. This, she realized, was why Eli was so eager to get the letter. The passage was "a special word to our black employees," the letter said. "It has come repeatedly to our attention that it is among you that the union supporters are making their most intensive drive—that you are being insistently told that the union is the wave of the future for you especially—and that by going into the union in mass, you can dominate it and control it in this plant, and in these Roanoke Rapids plants, as you may see fit," it said. Crystal Lee wrote rapidly, and angrily. It was not true what the letter said, she told herself. It was just that the black mill hands were not as afraid as the whites to openly join the union. But the whites would come around soon, she thought. "If now you become impatient and seek to create an organization in these plants consisting largely of your own race, it is our sincere belief that you will not be serving your own best interests," the letter said.

Eli had to know this, and quick, she thought. Crystal Lee knew whites far outnumbered blacks in the Stevens cotton mills in Roanoke Rapids. At the time she was copying the letter, barely 20 percent of JP's hands in the six cotton mills were blacks. And if JP could make the white workers who read this letter think the union was an all-black outfit, a black power outfit, then, Crystal Lee knew, the union could never win an election. She wrote faster, copying excerpts from the rest of the letter, and then she stopped. There was a man standing at her elbow.

It was Dave Moody, the assistant overseer. "Didn't I tell you last night you couldn't copy that letter?" he demanded of her.

"I know it, Dave, but I can't understand why. Y'all put it up there for me to read, and I'm going to copy it," Crystal Lee answered. She turned back to the bulletin board and started writing again. Moody said nothing more. He stepped back as a second man approached. It was James Alston, a general overseer, who was both Moody and Mabry's boss.

"Lee, you know you can't copy this letter," Alston said.

"James, I'm going to copy this letter. It's my break time, and I'm going to copy this letter," she said.

Alston reached out, as though to take Crystal Lee by the arm, and he said, "Lee, come on. Let's go to the office."

Crystal Lee turned on him. "No, James," she said. The smile on her face was gone now. "It's my break time, and I am going to copy this letter," she said.

Crystal Lee turned back to the bulletin board. She heard a third person walking up behind her, and when she turned around to see who this was, she found herself looking at the general supervisor of Delta #4, Mason Lee. He spoke her name.

"Well, Mr. Lee, I didn't know you knew my name," Crystal Lee said.

"I know you," the man answered. She looked him in the face a moment, then turned her back on him and began copying again. "Crystal, you are not going to copy this letter off this bulletin board," Lee said. She ignored him. "You are not going to copy this letter. You are going to leave," he said.

Crystal Lee whirled around. "You better not touch me," she told Lee. The three men took a step back. Moody and Alston looked at Mason Lee to see what he would do next.

"I'm going to call the police to come and take you out of this plant," Lee said.

She laughed at him then, and began to smile again, telling him, "Mr. Lee, I am going to finish copying this letter. And then, I am going to eat the supper."

She did just that. Perhaps none of the three bossmen had faced such defiance in a mill hand before, and the shock of it left them stunned and unable, momentarily, to make their next move. Or perhaps Crystal Lee's eyes held so much contempt, or hate, for those three bossmen, because they were bosses, they were men, and they were giving her orders, that they were afraid to do anything more just then.

Moody, Alston and Lee stood behind her as Crystal Lee finished copying the letter. No one spoke. When she finished, Crystal Lee folded her notes and stuck them in her bra, looking at the three men as she did so, and then walked back to her folding table, picked up her purse and joined the other mill hands in the safety-supper serving line. Tommy Gardner, the assistant general supervisor of Delta #4 and Mason Lee's chief aide, was serving the iced tea. Crystal Lee smiled at him as she went through the serving line and filled her plate, then joined her friends in the new canteen to eat. She took Mason Lee at his word, and expected to see the police enter the canteen any minute. She was smiling again, but behind the smile Crystal Lee was seething. "These bossmen, they've always held us back," she says. "They are the reason the cotton-mill workers are poor. A bossman says, 'These stupid fools coming in here, they got to work. This is about the only type of work they have.' And then the bossmen just run all over us, and run our lives, and this is what they want."

The police did not arrive while she ate. When she walked back on the shearing-room floor, Crystal Lee looked for a cop, expected to see one at her folding table, but there was no one there except the other women, already folding towels again. Crystal Lee redid her makeup, and was folding a towel when Dave

Moody appeared at her table. "Let's go to Mason Lee's office, Lee," he said. The two of them walked across the put-up department floor, not speaking to each other. As she walked toward the glass partition of the offices, Crystal Lee noticed the work floor was quiet. She learned later that word of her confrontation at the bulletin board had passed through the serving line, and the hands watched her now as Crystal Lee was taken from the work floor to face the bosses.

They were seated, waiting for her, when she walked into Lee's office. Melvia Reed, her forelady, was there. Dave Moody, Ray Mabry, James Alston, Tommy Gardner and Mason Lee were there. Lee spoke first. "Why did you use the pay phone on company time?" he asked. He must have meant when she had called Eli to complain about copying the letter, Crystal Lee thought, but she ignored Mason Lee's question. She had one of her own. From her purse she pulled out paper and pencil. She looked at Lee. "What's your full name and how do you spell it?" she asked him. Mason Lee's mouth dropped open. Before he could answer, however, Crystal Lee turned to his assistant, Tommy Gardner, and demanded of him: "What's your full name and how do you spell it?"

Mason Lee recovered then. He stood up, cut off Gardner with a motion before he could speak, then told Crystal Lee, "Look, we don't have to give you any of that." She dropped pencil and paper in her lap, put her hands over her ears, and closed her eyes. "Look, Mr. Lee, all of you people in here are against me. And I'm telling you, I'm not going to say anything until I have all of your names," she said.

Lee shouted at her: "I want you to leave this plant. Call your husband. Get him up here. Tell him to pick you up. I want you out of this plant now."

Crystal Lee did not move from her chair. She kept her eyes closed and her hands over her ears. "You're going to have to call the police to get me out of here," she said. "And you better make it the chief of police too," she said. "It better be Chief Drewery Beale to come get me. It better be him. It better not be any policeman. I've got a jealous husband, and he knows Drewery, and I can't just ride with anybody. Drewery Beale is my first cousin's husband, and he is the chief of police of Roanoke Rapids, and you better get him," she said.

Crystal Lee was about to cry, and she fought that, held back her tears. Tommy Gardner tried to calm her. "Look, Lee, let us call your husband for you," he said. "No," she told him. Then without another word, Crystal Lee stood up and walked out of the office. She walked across the open floor to her work table and stood there trying to keep control. She did not know what to expect next, nor what she should do next. Call Eli? Call Cookie?

She had no chance to do either. A Pinkerton guard was walking toward her. Crystal Lee stopped him ten feet from her table, before he said a word. "Look, man, I ain't going nowhere with you," she said. The security guard looked at her, shrugged, turned and left. Crystal Lee looked around the shearing-room floor. No one else was approaching her. The mill hands, she saw, had stopped their work. They were watching her. The room grew quieter. Behind her, Crystal Lee heard a door slam. She turned to it and saw a city policeman crossing the floor, heading toward her. It was not Chief Beale. She waited for the man to get closer to her, and then she shouted at him: "It's going to take you and the whole police department before you take me out of this mill."

The cop kept walking toward her. Crystal Lee backed to the edge of the folding table, felt it pressing on her back. She shouted again, "Mr. Lee said he was going to have the chief of police come in this mill and take me home, and I'm not going anywhere until the chief of police comes." She reached behind her on the table. The cop stopped where he was, ten feet from her. Crystal Lee kept looking at him as she pulled from the tabletop a sheet of stiff cardboard, one of the inserts used in packing. She picked up a black marking pencil from the table and began writing on the cardboard, in heavy, block letters. The cop came no closer. Crystal Lee hoisted herself onto the tabletop, then stood up on it. She held her sign high over her head, in both hands, and slowly turned in a circle so the mill hands on the open floor, the women in put-up, the side hemmers and terry cutters, all of them watching her now, could read what she had written: "UNION."

"I looked over the plant, and the hands was coming up like this, giving me the peace sign," Crystal Lee says.

She looked down and saw Ray Mabry standing at her table. The cop was with him, and so was her forelady, Melvia Reed. "Get down, Lee, come on down from there," Mabry said. Crystal Lee did not answer. She looked back over the open floor and kept moving her sign. Her sister, Syretha, was there on the floor, and she pleaded with Crystal Lee to get down. Crystal Lee's friend, the woman who had tried helping her copy the letter earlier that night, also begged her to stop. Crystal Lee kept turning her sign. She saw more mill hands holding their fists in the air, giving her V-for-victory signs, and doing it quietly, no shouts, no cheers, but quietly, standing by their machines, signaling to her. When she saw enough, Crystal Lee climbed down.

She looked past Mabry and Melvia Reed, past her sister and her friend, past the security guard and the city policeman, and saw coming through the door her cousin's husband, Chief Drewery Beale.

Chief Beale towered over the others. He wore a suit, and the unbuttoned coat gave Crystal Lee a glimpse of his pistol, holstered at his belt. "Lee, this doesn't have anything to do with the union," Beale said. Crystal Lee looked at him a long moment. She was about to ask if he had a warrant for her arrest, but she stopped. She did not care, any more, what the bossmen thought, or her sister, or what her friends in put-up thought of the police coming to arrest her. She thought then of Drewery Beale, who lived around the corner from her, who knew from his own wife about Jay's birth, who knew about the affair she had had later. She cared about what Drewery Beale was thinking, and she set her mouth and turned to him.

"I said to Drewery Beale, 'I'll tell you one thing: You're going to open that door for me to go out of here.' I said, 'I am a lady.' Because see," Crystal Lee says, "Drewery knows things. He knows me."

Chief Beale said nothing. No one else spoke. Crystal Lee went on: "Now, before I leave this spot right here, you're going to put in writing, 'I, Drewery Beale, will take Crystal Lee Jordan to 30 Henry Street.' Sign your name, and give me the note."

The bossmen looked at Beale in amazement. He was taking a sheet of paper from his notebook and starting to write on it. Then he stopped, jerked his head up, balled up the paper in his hand and flung it to the floor. "I don't have to do this; I don't have to write anything," he said. Beale turned to the bossmen.

Mason Lee was in the crowd at Crystal Lee's table now, and the chief said to him, "Do you want her off these premises?"

Mason Lee nodded. "Take her away," he said.

Chief Beale turned to Crystal Lee. He moved toward her, then he stopped. "I'm not going to get in that car with you by myself," he told her. Crystal Lee laughed. She smiled at Chief Beale, and she said to him, "Drewery, I'm not going to do anything to you."

Four of them walked off the floor: Crystal Lee, carrying her purse and her rug cushion, leading the way, and Chief Beale, and the cop, Lieutenant Harry Vaughn, and the Pinkerton guard following in a line behind her.

Chief Beale opened the plant door for her, and as Crystal Lee walked by him and out into the night she said to Beale, "Drewery, you think you know me. But I know you. You are going to take me home." Beale did not answer her. The Pinkerton guard dropped behind, and Crystal Lee, the chief and Lieutenant Vaughn passed through the gate in the chain-link fence. Two cars were parked at the curb, the one in front of Crystal Lee a new, unmarked car with paper dealer's tags on it, and the other, thirty feet behind the first car, a standard police cruiser. Crystal Lee did not know which car they would put her in, nor who owned the unmarked car. Again she took pencil and paper from her purse, this time to write down the tag number of the unmarked car. She began wondering if Beale and Vaughn would take her home. Nobody had said she was under arrest, she thought, but neither had Beale said he would take her home. It struck her, for the first time that night, that she might go to jail, that JP wanted her thrown in jail, and that once she got in that car, Beale would not take her home, but take her to jail instead.

Crystal Lee dropped her paper and pencil. She spun around, saw Vaughn locking the gate, took half a step toward him, then jumped at the gate, dropping her purse and the rug, gripping the chain-link fence with her fingers. "No you don't," Vaughn shouted. He heaved the gate closed, jerking Crystal Lee back, but her grip on the weave of the fence held her to it. "It's too late for that. You're going to jail and not back in there," Vaughn shouted. Crystal Lee gripped the heavy wire as tightly as she could. She felt strong hands on her arms and saw Beale pulling her back. Vaughn grabbed her hands and began prying her fingers out of the fence. She could not hold on. The two men wrenched her away from the gate, turned her around, and holding her by the arms rushed her ahead of them to the police cruiser. They stuffed her in the back and slammed the door. There were no door handles, no window cranks, in the back seat of the cruiser. A thick wire mesh separated Crystal Lee from the front seat. "I felt like I was suffocating," she says.

Vaughn and Beale got in the front seat. In silence, each man breathing heavily from the short, fierce struggle at the gate, they drove away from the mill. It was her last chance to plead to be taken home and not to jail, but Crystal Lee said nothing. She looked out the window, saw the low roof of Delta #4 pass, then the high, dark bulk of the Rosemary mill, its bricked-in windows letting no light out in the darkness. The cruiser turned right at 10th Street and Crystal Lee knew then she was on her way to jail. She went in silence. They drove past the Motel Dixie, and Crystal Lee thought of Eli there, and then they turned off 10th Street onto Roanoke Avenue and drove down that dark, silent street to the city jail.

Chief Beale led her inside. They went to the magistrate's office first. Crystal Lee saw a couch in the corner and she went to it, looked at Beale, then lay down on the couch. Beale swore out a warrant for her arrest. According to the criminal history card on file she was processed into jail as "Jordan, Chrystal [misspelled] Pulley, 30 Henry Street, Roanoke Rapids, female, white, 32, occupation textile, fair complexion, brown hair, gray eyes." Her arrest number was 6147-D, and the charge against her was disorderly conduct.

A jail matron came to the door, and Beale motioned for Crystal Lee to follow the woman. She led Crystal Lee through a narrow, winding corridor, its walls painted pale green, its steps barely discernible in the dark shadows thrown by a single naked lightbulb in the corridor. They walked by the drunk tank, empty that night, past more empty cells, through a small courtyard where Crystal Lee glimpsed stars in the night overhead, and then to two adjoining cells, the women's section. Crystal Lee had not spoken since Beale and Vaughn had forced her into the car. She even refused to give her name when booked. She did not speak to the matron, and the matron did not speak to her. The cell door clanged shut behind her, and Crystal Lee was left alone.

Her cell was ten feet long and five feet wide, and the ceiling was far overhead, more than fifteen feet. A single bulb in the corridor beyond the bars lit her cell. Two narrow bunk beds hung by chains from the wall. There was a toilet, a washbasin and nothing else. "I was beginning to get a little scared, knowing they might come in and search me and find all these union notes on me," Crystal Lee says. The matron had not searched her then, and Crystal Lee still had in her bra the notes she had taken when she copied the letter. "I took these notes out of my bra, and I tore them up and wrapped them in tissue paper and put them in the commode," she says. As she was flushing it, Chief Beale and the matron came to her cell door. She had the right to make one phone call, Beale said, and she could make it now.

Back through the courtyard and the long corridor the three went, to a desk sergeant's phone. Crystal Lee did not call her husband. She dialed the Motel Dixie instead and asked for Eli Zivkovich. His room did not answer. She asked the motel operator to ring Margaret Bank's room, room eight, and she got an answer then.

"It was about nine o'clock when the phone rings," Eli remembers. "It was Margaret Banks and she said, 'Eli, we got problems. Crystal Jordan's been fired and she's in jail.' I told Margaret I'd be right there. Then I called Harold McIver in Charlotte to find out about bond money in case I didn't have that kind of money, and he said chances are they'll release her, and if not, he'd get the bond money to us."

Crystal Lee had not told Margaret Banks why she was in jail, and when Banks and Eli arrived at the city jail Chief Beale had them sent to him in his office. Eli had never met Beale. "I told him why I was here. Got the details. He said she had misbehaved, resisted arrest, and tried to break away and what have you. He was nice to me, to Margaret, and I says, 'Let me go back and talk to her.' I went back and offered her a cigarette. She told me she didn't smoke. I didn't know whether she smoked or not. And she's laying on that sack crying, scared to death. I told the chief that I was here to get her released, so I signed a recognizance, and that was it. I don't recall Crystal Lee saying anything. The girl was scared. She'd never been in jail, and God knows what her husband's going to do to her, you know. I figured the only thing was to bring her back to the motel room, and I told her to call her husband from there," Eli says.

Crystal Lee stopped crying when she left the jail. She sat alone in the back seat of Eli's car as the three drove to the Motel Dixie. Eli still could not understand what she had done. The chief gave him the details, but he found it hard to believe Crystal Lee had gone so far, had taken such a hard stand against the bossmen, and against the police. If he had known what was coming, Eli thought, he would have told Crystal Lee to forget the letter, that he'd get it another way. Eli glanced at her and frowned. He was not at all certain, he decided then, just what Crystal Lee had done that night, and he did not think it was something she did just for the union.

From Eli's motel room, Crystal Lee phoned Cookie at home. "I'm over here at the Motel Dixie, in room seven, and would you go get someone to keep the children and come over here?" she told him.

Cookie had just finished cleaning the dishes from dinner. He and the three children were watching television. "I could tell by the tone of her voice she was really upset. I was stunned. I was shocked. I didn't know what in the world she was doing at the Dixie Motel," Cookie says. "First thing that popped into my mind, I said, 'Well, I'm walking into something I don't really know what I'm facing. I don't know what I got in store for me up there.' So the first thing I thought, I said, 'Well, I better take my gun, in case something does pop up I won't be in such bad shape.' "

Cookie left the children watching television. He drove rapidly to Syretha's house, where one of her older daughters agreed to come stay with the Jordan children. Back home, Cookie went to the bedroom and pulled his pistol out of its hiding place. He slipped it into his pants pocket, in front, and walked out the back door to his car. The gun was Cookie's .38 caliber revolver, the same pistol he had once taken to hunt down his first wife and her lover, the same pistol he had taken to go talk to Crystal Lee's lover, and now, for all he knew, he thought, the same old scene faced him again.

When he turned into the Motel Dixie parking lot, Cookie had the car lights off. He did not check at the desk to find room seven, but instead quietly walked by the doors of the motel wing nearest him. He found room seven, felt his pants pocket for the pistol, and knocked on the door.

"Yeah, goddam. Cookie came in. He came bouncing in there, and I said, 'Now, settle down now,'" Eli says. Crystal Lee was lying on the bed fully clothed. Margaret Banks sat in a chair by one of the desks, and Eli stood at the foot of the bed. The two men, who had never met, looked at each other. "Eli right away wanted to tell me what had happened, and he went on to tell me that the police had come to the mill up there, had taken my wife, locked her in jail. They were taking her statement of what had happened. It upset me. It really did upset me, not knowing all of it," Cookie says. Gradually, however, he realized that this was not the scene he had been rehearsing over and over again in his mind. He had not been cuckolded again, and he relaxed. "Well, I looked and sized the situation up. I saw Eli and Margaret there, and I knew right away, I said to myself, 'Well, ain't nothing here I can't handle,'" Cookie says.

Eli assured him the union would take Crystal Lee's case, and that the police were wrong. He listened to Eli's account of the five hours Crystal Lee had spent in the cotton mill that night, and he nodded occasionally. Like Eli, Cookie could not understand why his wife had taken things so far. He knew that he, Cookie Jordan, would never have done that. Crystal Lee had not spoken, had let Eli tell her story for her while she watched Cookie from the bed. When Eli finished, the room was still. Margaret, Eli and Cookie looked at her. Crystal Lee was no longer the woman they knew. Her defiance that night had freed her from the cotton mills and, through them, from the mill-hand life that pushed her and pulled her however she fought it. It had done more than that, though, and the others knew it as well as she did. She had risked more than they, and the act had left her free, and alone.

6

ON WEDNESDAY, JUNE 6, one week after she had been fired, Crystal Lee Jordan gathered her family together in the living room at 30 Henry Street.

"I took my three children, Mark, Jay, and Elizabeth, and my husband was in the room, and I sit down, and I told them the story of my life," she says.

First, she told her children she loved them. She said she loved Cookie, sitting there, and he loved her. Then, for the first time, she told Mark that his real father was Junior Wood, who died four months after Mark was born. She told Jay she had never married his father, who was not Cookie, not Junior, but another man. And she told Elizabeth and the boys that she had had an affair with a fourth man shortly after Elizabeth was born. Crystal Lee began to cry as she told her children this, and soon they were crying too.

As she spoke, she held in her lap an old small lockbox she had brought from her bedroom.

"This file box that I kept locked up—I had pictures of Jay's father in there. I had a few pictures of Mark's father. And I told them, 'I know y'all have always wondered why I wouldn't let you go in this box.' I had the settlement papers on Jay that was made between me and his father. I said, 'These are not for me.' I said, 'Jay, this is your stuff.' I said, 'It's not mine, it's yours. It's your life.' I said, 'I want you to always feel like there's nothing that you cannot come to me and talk to me about. Any problems, any way in the world I can help you. You know what your life is. You know what your mother is. This is all I can do for you,'" she said.

She was telling them all this, Crystal Lee said to her children, because she was changing her life, already had started to in fact, and it was bound to affect them. If they became mill hands, she said, then she wanted life to be better for them than it had been for her. So, she said, she had joined the union, and because of that she had been fired, and now, she said, the people who opposed the union might try to use this story against her, even try to turn the children against her.

"Someday somebody is going to be cruel enough that they are going to tell these things. So I think it was my place and my duty to tell them myself," Crystal Lee says. "I told my children, I said, 'I'm not making any excuses for myself.' I said, 'Just like everyone else, I'm not perfect, and I made these mistakes. I hope that y'all will learn from my experiences that life has a meaning; there is a moral reason for why you should do this, and why you shouldn't do this.'"

Crystal Lee had wondered for days whether or not

she should tell the children. She asked Eli Zivkovich about it, and in doing that, she told Eli her story as well. Crystal Lee talked with Cookie about it too. "I have put him through a lot of hell," she says of her husband. "I have shamed him. Don't you think that people haven't made smart remarks to him about his wife because they know these things?" she says.

"This has involved my entire personal life. It has made me reveal things to my children that I was afraid someone else would. Every day since I became pregnant with Jay, my life has been tormented. Every day there's not a second that went by that I didn't fear that someone would tell my children. You can imagine every day for almost thirteen years, thinking about these things. All this time I have wanted to tell them. Now, I have cleaned out my closet. My children know what I am, but they also know that I am an honest woman, and I believe in standing up for my rights," she says.

Crystal Lee had time on her hands now, and she offered to the union, and to Eli, the hours of the day she once spent folding towels for JP. She had been fired, jailed, and revealed, by herself, before her children, and all of it made even greater Crystal Lee's personal stake in the outcome of Eli's campaign. The way she chose to stand up for her rights, fighting back at once as she did, considering that she was a mill hand, and a woman, surprised many of the union officials. Some of them were leery of Crystal Lee, and considered her unpredictable. Eli found this out before Crystal Lee did.

"One of the investigators from the NLRB had a cook-out at his place outside town right after Crystal Lee was fired," Eli says. "When I got there, his first comment was, 'Where is that stripper that got up on the table and hootchy-kootchied and all?' " Eli looked upon the investigator as a union sympathizer, and was puzzled by his attitude. He was disappoined to notice the same attitude in Harold McIver, the IUD organizing chief and Eli's boss, when Eli took Crystal Lee to Charlotte the next week to file charges against JP for firing her.

The disorderly-conduct charges against her were dropped by Chief Beale, largely because neither the city nor the police department wanted to side openly with JP in what was likely to become another federal court case. Nor did JP need to prosecute Crystal Lee. She had been fired, perhaps even humiliated, and the union with her, by being led away in police custody. Eli, however, wanted the union to take Crystal Lee's case to the NLRB and federal court, in part to win back her job, and in larger part to show the other mill hands that Crystal Lee could have it back if she wanted, that JP could not beat the union by firing union sympathizers.

"We went down and talked with McIver, and he assured us that everything would be done that could possibly be done to defend her," Eli says. "But I had to convince Harold that she had a case. He thought she was insubordinate. It's this whole Southern bit. And how many good cases have been dismissed on that very misnomer? You know damn well it's not a question of insubordination. This is just the first thing that comes to a Southerner's mind if you don't obey. But it wasn't that way. It was a girl doing what she was legally entitled to do. And she gets fired for it."

Eli managed to hide from Crystal Lee the union's doubts about her case, but he could not hide the fact that the union was wary toward her. If the union failed to learn a lesson from the bitterness left by its not taking care of the three women fired in its last Roanoke Rapids campaign, Eli had learned. He insisted Crystal Lee be hired as an organizer, not only for the help she could give the campaign, but also to replace the wages she had lost when JP fired her. McIver reluctantly agreed to put Crystal Lee on the TWUA payroll at $110 a week. But he added a condition. No one else, not her friends in the mills, not other union members, was to know the union was paying Crystal Lee.

The union wanted her wages kept secret, Crystal Lee eventually learned, not because her work was unappreciated, nor because she had been fired, nor even because she had borne a child out of wedlock and had had an affair. It was just that the union wished she had not been so open about it all. How would it look to the rest of the mill hands in Roanoke Rapids? And what might JP say to its workers about a union with a paid organizer who had that kind of personal story to tell?

Eli did not care about Crystal Lee's past. He did not ignore it, but accepted it, and Crystal Lee felt comfortable with him because of that. Eli did not yet feel confident in his knowledge of the mills, the town, or the workers, and he still needed to enlist white workers in the union campaign. He needed Crystal Lee to do that. That summer of 1973 she spent more than eight hours a day working with Eli. Cookie seemed to understand and accept Crystal Lee's union work then. "She believes that it can be a help to the labor movement, and it might save somebody from doing what she did, some young girl. It might save her from having the troubles that she's had. That is the reason she did it," Cookie says. He accepted Eli too, because, "Eli can really turn you on. And, he's sincere, and he believes in what he's doing. He believes it. Every little thing that happened was important to Eli."

The union campaign in Roanoke Rapids that summer appeared more than once to be as much Eli and Crystal Lee's campaign as it was the TWUA's. Eli and Crystal Lee faced an enormous task in changing the habits and dispelling the fears that were a way of life in Roanoke Rapids. Eli was awake at six every morning, and rarely went to sleep before two the next morning. Crystal Lee kept nearly the same grueling schedule. There were shift changes to meet, at midnight, eight in the morning, and four in the afternoon, and leaflets to be handed out then. "But, hell, I wasn't sent there to wait," Eli says of the early days in the campaign.

His bosses in the union told him to make house calls on the workers, to use Crystal Lee's contacts to visit homes and persuade the mill hands in one-to-one conversations to join the union. "House-calling seems to be a disease with TUWA, that it's the only way you're going to organize. Hell, how could we make house calls on thirty-seven hundred workers?" Eli says. Instead, Eli outlined his own strategy to Crystal Lee, one that, if it worked, would let them call for, and win, an election by late fall. They would recruit an organizing committee of mill hands still working for JP. They would be volunteers, talking for the union both inside the brick walls while they worked, and throughout the town when they were not working for JP. They would have to be tough, because JP would pressure them once the company identified the leaders, as Eli was certain it would. At least half of them had to be white. Then, Eli hoped, that core of workers would enlist other mill hands, like a chain reaction, who in turn would enlist still more. He would have the workers' committee meet weekly, and any problems they could not deal with themselves, Eli would take on. And he would continue the weekly rallies, to keep enthusiasm high, hoping a gradual swelling of the union ranks, openly gathering in the heart of Roanoke Rapids in the middle of a Sunday afternoon, would attract still more mill hands.

Crystal Lee and Eli found JP's opposition, and influence, all over town that summer. "We used the black church three times before word got to me that the white people would not come to it," Eli says. When they tried to find a white church for union rallies, the white ministers turned them down. Eli's weekly report to the Charlotte offices on July 21 noted the resistance: "Stevens began changing working conditions in plants, adding more looms to a worker in a stretchout, and reducing the work week, and through that the wages, of union members. Major problem getting whites in campaign."

Even Crystal Lee, who grew up in cotton-mill towns and thought she knew all there was to know about bossmen fighting the union, saw anti-union tactics new to her. She learned about two Southern law firms known for fighting unions: Constangy & Prowell of Atlanta, and Blakeney, Alexander & Machon of Charlotte. "That's the Constangy defense," she said, or, "That's the Blakeney resistance," as she learned to spot the techniques. She saw anti-union letters mailed to the workers that included this paragraph: "You may not have noticed in the newspapers that the AFL-CIO at its recent convention took $75,000 of the dues paid to it by the people who are its members and gave this money to the National Association for the Advancement of Colored People, which is the organization aggressively working for the wiping out of all racial segregation, both in schools, manufacturing plants and elsewhere."

In the parking lots around JP's mills, Crystal Lee picked up discarded copies of a newspaper she'd never seen before, *The Militant Truth*, and read fiery stories accusing unions of fostering communism and promoting the "mongrelization of the races." She began to be a little worried.

Eli shrugged off her worries, and Crystal Lee admired him more and more that summer, seeing in Eli more strength and courage than she had in almost any other man. She worked hard to win his respect, to please him, bringing to his motel room more and more white mill hands. Eli was so competent, Crystal Lee thought. He always seemed to her to be able to take care of anything, and so, when she found a troubled young mill hand, a white man with a confession to make, she took the man to Eli, certain Eli would accept the confession just as Eli had accepted hers.

Crystal Lee sat in Eli's room while the young man told Eli that in the union's last campaign he signed an anti-union statement, and JP used it against the union. Eli kept his reservations to himself and accepted the man. If the young man truly had changed, it would not hurt to have a six-foot-five, 250-pound white mill hand at his side, Eli thought. The man was jubilant. He turned his station wagon into a union float, with banners, pennants and United States flags in front and back and a huge sign on top: "I'm for TWUA."

"Then, I'll be damned if he doesn't turn around and carry news back to the company," Eli says. The young mill hand had suggested to his foreman that he forge names on union membership cards, hundreds of them, to make Eli think he had more support than he actually did. Eli learned about the ruse from another mill hand, and confronted the young man the next time he came to the motel. They were standing in front of the door to Eli's room. Crystal Lee was inside, watching. Eli took the man's organizing card out of the file and tore it up in front of him. The huge mill hand stared at Eli in disbelief. He opened his mouth, closed it, opened it and closed it, and no words came out, just a guttural, stuttering noise. He began to tremble. He turned from Eli and stomped across the parking lot to his station wagon. He took the union sign on top, a sign four feet by eight feet and made of wood and cardboard, and tore it to pieces with his hands. He ripped off the banners and pennants and flung the flags on the blacktop. Then he reached through a window to the glove compartment, got something in his hand that Eli could not see, and stomped back across the parking lot to Eli's door.

"He shoved a bullet in my gut, a slug. And I looked at him and said, 'Man, you can't do it that way. What you've got to do is put that thing in a chamber, then you got to point that daggoned thing at the guy and pull the trigger, and then you do it.' And I handed the slug back to him," Eli says. Crystal Lee saw it all from inside the room. With such a man at her side, a man like Eli, who could stand up to that giant, who was not even angry with her for bringing the young mill hand to the motel in the first place, Crystal Lee began to believe she could do more than just win a union campaign. Who could touch her now? Not JP, she thought, because she no longer cared whether or not she ever worked in the mills again. The mills had nothing she wanted. Not anyone or anything in her past, she thought, because she already had opened up her past for everyone to see. Not Cookie, she thought, because he must know by now that she was a woman who set her own course. No one in Roanoke Rapids could stop her, Crystal Lee thought.

She was turning out to be Eli's chief aide, far more valuable to him, in fact, than Margaret Banks, who had been hired as Eli's equal. "The time Crystal Lee put into that campaign was awesome," Eli says. "Like, it meant catching people late at night, catching them a half-hour before they go to work, this kind of thing. And we met a pile of people that wouldn't mind seeing you at that hour because they think nobody's going to see that union man at my house at that hour, and it opened doors, and eventually brought them to meetings, brought them to the office. And Crystal Lee was the example. There was no way that anyone could back off after talking to her. I'd just tell them, 'If you've got half the guts that she's got, you're going to make it.' She was the Mother Jones of the textile union.* A good example was the beautiful job she did when I had to go to Cheraw one week. Hell, she picked up fifty cards that week we were gone, and she took statements, discrimination cases that are still in the hands of the labor board, still alive. She did that where Margaret Banks couldn't do it, and where I couldn't really count on the other workers to do it. She was quick to grasp and know what it was all about."

Crystal Lee introduced Eli to white mill hands who became members of his in-plant organizing committee. Even Cookie, who tried to avoid the TWUA campaign as much as possible, recognized the work Crystal Lee was doing. "She could get Eli in to meet the people that otherwise it would be impossible to get by," he says. "And she wasn't timid or afraid to go and meet whoever. And she wasn't scared about what the next-

*Mother Jones was a heroine of early coal-mine organizing in West Virginia.

door neighbor was gonna say because she had visited some black family, or had a black family in our home to talk about union. It didn't bother her. It didn't bother me. If it had ever bothered me, I'd a said, 'Uh-uh, no. Do it up there at the union hall if you're gonna do it. Get out of the house.' But she was honest, and she was sincere in her desire to help the union come in here. She believed in it wholeheartedly."

Cookie insisted that summer that blacks in his home did not bother him, that Crystal Lee's union work did not bother him, that he was proud of her. But he had doubts about it, keeping them to himself, letting them gnaw inside him. Innuendoes began to circulate in town about Crystal Lee and Eli spending so much time together in that room at the Motel Dixie, being together late into the night while Cookie worked at the paper mill. By September, the gossip about Eli and Crystal Lee had reached the two of them, the union chiefs in Charlotte, and Cookie. "I may have, at one time, thought that them working so close, that an attraction could be between them," Cookie said. "But that came about because of the part that Lee was put in in the organizing campaign. Eli just got to the point where, when he needed anything done, when he needed to know any information about anybody, about the mill, he'd say, 'Crystal, do you know so and so?' And she'd say, 'Yeah, I know him. I know where it is. I know his wife. I know about this, and I know about this, and I know about that.' And that was the reason that Eli wanted her to work with him so closely. There wasn't anything more than that."

Eli's union bosses were not so placid. They told Eli to move out of the Motel Dixie, to find another place for the campaign headquarters, and Eli found a vacant storefront office on Roanoke Avenue. But he began to wonder just how his bosses heard that gossip, who in Roanoke Rapids told them, and why.

All of Crystal Lee's life, from what Eli knew of it, seemed to have been one crisis after another, usually involving a man. "Crystal Lee is a very provocative type of person, and there could have been stuff taking place that I didn't know anything about: the constant jealousies and what not, her baring of the soul," Eli says. "I don't know. These are just suspicions on my part, and I couldn't care less about them as long as they're not affecting the campaign." Not a hint of Eli's doubts about her ever reached Crystal Lee. Had she known of them, she might have withdrawn from the union campaign in anger, her feelings hurt because Eli did not give her the complete trust she gave him. Crystal Lee was positive she had learned to control that urge within her to console, and help, and inevitably become painfully involved with those certain men who seemed helpless on their own, whose troubles made her want to take such men into her arms, to patch them up, make them whole again, and send them away after they no longer needed her so much. Perhaps she had learned to control that. She also believed, and this much seemed even more certain, that the days of casual affairs, of men in her life such as Ira Stonehouse, were behind her. Eli believed that much too. But perhaps he sensed in Crystal Lee the presence of her other compulsion.

Eli wondered whether the gossip about Crystal Lee and himself originated with Margaret Banks. He did know she did not like Crystal Lee, nor Crystal Lee her, and he knew, as well, that Banks could have her own valid reasons for disliking him. There was, for example, the daily reality of seeing Eli praise Crystal Lee's work in the campaign, and ignore her own.

Morale in the campaign was on the point of collapse by October, Eli thought, and on October 28, at Eli's insistence, the union transferred Margaret Banks out of town.

One of the things Crystal Lee always wanted to be, but never could, was a cheerleader. She told Eli once that she had never bothered to try out for cheerleader in high school because she thought she came from the wrong part of town, the mill village part. Early that fall, Crystal Lee suggested to Eli that the union campaign have its own cheerleaders. She would organize them, she said, buy material with union money, sew the outfits herself: red skirts lined with white, red shorts, white sweat shirts with red TWUA letters sewed on, white knee socks and little red and white pompoms with bells in them on the shoes. Eli agreed.

Elizabeth, Crystal Lee and Cookie's eight-year-old daughter, was the first cheerleader. By Christmas of 1973, Crystal Lee had recruited thirty girls between the ages of eight and sixteen. They practiced every Friday night in the karate-club studio on Roanoke Avenue. Crystal Lee took her cheerleader corps to the state fair in Raleigh that fall, and to union rallies in Cheraw and Aberdeen. The girls, half of them white, half of them black, wrote their own cheers. "Extra, extra, read all about it. We got a union, and there's no doubt about it," was one. Another, which Elizabeth wrote, was, "You can knock us; you can shock us; you can lay down flat. But tell me Stevens, can you beat that?"

As good an idea for boosting morale as the cheerleaders proved to be, it too led to another quarrel involving Crystal Lee. One of the cheerleaders, a sixteen-year-old girl, wanted to be in charge of the group, and her mother was a member of Eli's in-plant committee of organizers. Crystal Lee refused to give up her role, and Eli supported her again, saying he wanted an older woman to chaperone the cheerleaders. The argument left one more jealous woman in the campaign ranks.

Little that Eli did seemed to alleviate the bickering around and about Crystal Lee. Little that she herself did seemed to be exempt from jealousy. Crystal Lee felt the tense withdrawal of others around her, of all except Eli, but she would not allow herself to be drawn into a fight. A sarcastic comment from another mill hand in the campaign only made her more determined to work still harder. Eli, however, could not ignore it. The jealousies between Crystal Lee and other women in the campaign seemed to have no end, recognize no limits. One of the women in the campaign went so far as to tell him that Crystal Lee had a starring role, along with a member of the city police force, in a locally produced, pornographic, explicit stag film. The movie was being shown at a lodge on Lake Gaston west of Roanoke Rapids, a lodge owned by a merchant in town, she claimed. "If you don't believe me, I'll get my son to bring you a copy of it," the woman told Eli. He had told her, "You do that," and then Eli forgot about it. The woman had not produced a copy of the film, had not mentioned it since that conversation, so Eli was taken by surprise when the gossip came up again. This time a new member of his staff, Peter Galladet, hired to replace Margaret Banks, brought up the story. "Are you sure you checked it out?" he asked Eli.

Galladet, young and inexperienced in union work,

nevertheless had earned Eli's respect as a hard worker. Eli knew, too, that Galladet and Crystal Lee were cool to each other. Eli noticed that, but did not act on it, did not realize that Crystal Lee felt the campaign belonged to her and to Eli, felt the two of them alone would win it, and resented the arrival of any other union organizer. Eli moved quickly to put an end to the stag-film gossip. He phoned the merchant, and he phoned the policeman who supposedly was in the film, and he asked for an immediate meeting. He told both men on the phone what he had been told about the film, and both men agreed at once to meet at the merchant's house that night.

"Look, I'm not here to mince words," Eli said when the three men sat down together. "I'm here on a very serious matter." The merchant and the cop denied the gossip. The merchant's wife, who joined the three men in the living room, said the story was absurd. Their denials convinced Eli there was nothing to the story. But he had not liked being forced to disclose to strangers, to the cop and the grocer, the internal bickering of his campaign. He began to feel that soon it would no longer matter whether or not Crystal Lee was in any way to blame for the gossip and dissension around her. However innocent she might be, Eli felt his first obligation was to the campaign, his campaign, and his determination to show this slow, timid union how JP could be beaten. Four weeks later, even though it was not Crystal Lee who started it, there was another fight, a real one this time.

Crystal Lee persuaded Eli to rent a float for the union cheerleaders to ride in the annual Roanoke Rapids Christmas parade. Like the cheerleaders, Crystal Lee told Eli, the float would help identify the union with the community. Eight cheerleaders were on the float, and the rest in formation behind it. On both sides the float had the message, "Good Tidings and Merry Christmas from the Textile Workers Union of America." The float was parked in a vacant lot, the parade assembly point, and Cookie, who had volunteered to pull the float, had just backed his car to it. Then across the lot and up to the float came another car, a station wagon driven by the same big mill hand Eli had argued with in August. He was going to pull the float, he said to Eli, because he was tired of the Jordan family getting all the glory in this campaign. The young man backed his car next to Cookie's, then began to hitch the float to the bumper. Cookie stepped up to him and said, "I'm pulling the damn thing." The big mill hand put his hand on Cookie's shoulder, as though to brush him back, and Cookie slugged him in the jaw. The young man struck right back, a glancing blow off Cookie's arm and forehead, and then Eli stepped between the two men. Eli threatened to call the police if the young man did not leave.

Two days later, Crystal Lee and Peter Galladet started arguing in the union office, and Eli finally lost his patience. "I've had it," he said to Crystal Lee. "Get the hell out of the office." It was a harsh, and hard, step for Eli to take and he said later, "I tried to tell her that I had to do it. I didn't want people who were doing work not to do work because they'd be irritated with her presence. You keep the ship together however the best you know."

Crystal Lee took her banishment with uncharacteristic stoicism, but Cookie, keeping to himself the jealous suspicions he had of Crystal Lee and Eli, took this as his chance to tell her she should have listened to him earlier. "I told my wife, after that first meeting, Eli spotted her," Cookie says. "It's not that Eli had it set up for her to be fired and all this. But it was intended to happen that way. The way I figure it, now Eli could just sense the interest she had in the union. He could sense it. She's a strong-willed person. And it's just like I told her. I feel like that she was picked, out of all those people up there, she was picked to play the part that she's playing. This damn stuff just didn't happen. I mean it just didn't just happen for no reason at all," Cookie says.

But Crystal Lee refused to complain. "I got mad, but I didn't say anything to Eli," she says. She had found, since that night in May when she was fired by JP, that she could control her anger, her Pulley temper, more easily than before. Cutting her ties with the cotton mills, she believed, had made her stronger, not weaker, had helped her see she did not need the mills. There was a calmness within her too; she had felt it since the day she had opened her past before her children. Within a week of being sent into exile, Crystal Lee was back at work on the campaign. She avoided the union office on Roanoke Avenue, but she and Eli remained a team, meeting shifts at the gates and visiting mill hands' homes at night. She was still on the union payroll. Eli had purposely said nothing to the Charlotte union offices about ordering Crystal Lee out of the office. Cookie could not understand why Crystal Lee stayed in the campaign. "Four or five hours a day she spent going door to door, and then it got to the point she was spending more time campaigning, a whole lot more time, than she was spending at home. I mean, she was just coming home to sleep. She got so involved that I feel that she felt like she was the only one that could really bring the union victory about, she and Eli," Cookie said.

Crystal Lee did feel that way, and so did Eli. Both

of them, in fact, were convinced they were on the verge of winning. All their steady, quiet hours of talking to the mill hands, visiting homes, holding Sunday rallies, were paying off. By December, almost two thousand mill hands had signed union membership cards. Even if a fourth of those switched back to JP's side in the last days before an election, which was what Eli predicted would happen, the union still had enough votes to win. Eli's reports to Charlotte warned his union boses that now was the time to call for a vote, that the mill hands were stirring, and this moment could easily pass them by. His in-plant organizing force included fifty-two men and women in Delta #4, Crystal Lee's old mill, fifty-five in Rosemary mill, fifty-nine in Patterson, twenty-eight in Roanoke #2. But Harold McIver of the IUD in Charlotte, and Paul Swaity, the TWUA organizing director, and Sol Stettin, the TWUA president, getting their reports in the union's New York headquarters, continued to stall. They told Eli the campaign was not yet solid enough, not strong enough to assure a victory. Not until four months later, on April 21, after a Sunday rally in the paperworkers' hall where the out-of-town union leaders saw first-hand the enthusiastic determination of the mill hands, did the TWUA finally agree to have an election held by the National Labor Relations Board to determine if JP's 3,700 mill hands in Roanoke Rapids would be represented by the union. The decision came one year after Eli went to work for the union and began the campaign in Roanoke Rapids, and eleven months after Crystal Lee joined Eli's campaign. By the time the election was held, both Crystal Lee and Eli would be observers only.

All through late January, February and early March, Cookie had brooded about Crystal Lee's union work.

There were small arguments between him and Crystal Lee about the union, the campaign, and her hours away from home.

Their quarreling drew in Eli, who tried to explain away Cookie's doubts, not realizing that Cookie considered Eli responsible for this change in his home, his family, and his wife. "I was playing it by ear with those two, rolling with it day in and day out," Eli says. "I talked with Cookie so many times it isn't funny. I said, 'Look, Cookie, don't do anything to hurt the campaign.' I was always worried that he might do something, I don't know what, that would hurt the campaign," Eli says.

Crystal Lee and Cookie's fighting steadily grew worse. Crystal Lee knew a showdown was coming. As far as she was concerned, the fight began the night she was fired, when Cookie saw her in Eli's motel room and heard Eli's account of what she had done. "Cookie just couldn't see how important the campaign was to me. And he got mad at me when I wanted to continue helping the union after they had done nothing for me," she says. Worst of all, Crystal Lee said, "Cookie was afraid I had finally freed myself, that he was going to lose me."

On March 15, a Friday night, Crystal Lee and Cookie's long quarrel broke open. It was past eleven o'clock and the children were in bed. Cookie and Crystal Lee were sitting at the kitchen table at 30 Henry Street when he started it. He had had it with her union work, and had it with her being gone all day and half the night, he said. He wanted her home, with the children. "I don't think you ought to fight in front of the children," Crystal Lee began to say. Cookie cut her off. "The children. How the hell can you talk about the children when you never see them?" he said.

That stab about the children hurt her. In the end, she thought, the whole point of her union work, of the union itself, was the children: so life in the mills would be better for them than it had been for her if they went to work for JP. She decided to show Cookie right then that nothing he said would take her away from the union campaign, away from what she believed, on her own, was the right thing for her to do. "Look, Cookie, I'm going to go down to the paper plant tomorrow and see if I can't get me some of those men sitting around with their own union protecting them, and get them to come help us get a union," she said. "They could pass out leaflets, come to meetings, do anything," she went on. Suddenly Cookie shouted back at her, "The hell you say, the hell you say. I dare you to go down there in front of those men. I don't want no wife of mine doing that. You do that and you can get the hell out of this house. I want you out of that union right now. I want you at home. That union ain't done nothing for you, and it ain't done nothing for us, and I want you out of it starting now, or you can get out of this house."

Cookie was standing now, his face and neck red with anger, his body shaking as he looked down at Crystal Lee. "I thought he had got to the point then that he was so worked up that he might kill me," Crystal Lee says. Cookie had just one more thing to tell her, he said then: "You're in love with Eli. That's right, ain't it?" Crystal Lee said her last words of the night to Cookie then, talking to Cookie's back as he turned and walked out of the kitchen to go to bed alone: "I love Eli Zivkovich like a father, and that's it."

The next day, Saturday, Crystal Lee packed her and the children's clothes and left the house while Cookie was at work. She and the children moved in with her sister, Syretha, then went to stay with friends, and finally, Crystal Lee left Roanoke Rapids to search for a new place to live, another job and another start, in the cotton mills of Burlington.

On Monday, May 13, Eli Zivkovich drove to the airport in Richmond, Virginia, to pick up Stettin, the TWUA president, and Swaity, the union's organizing director. Eli wanted the two men as his captive audience in the car during the two-hour drive back to Roanoke Rapids. He had persuaded them to come to a rally that night, to boost the campaign for the election that would be held in August. But what he secretly hoped would happen was that the TWUA would finally accept his reasoning that JP could never be unionized unless the giant chain was taken on in every Southern town where it had a mill. Eli talked of nothing else on the trip. He warned that JP, should it lose the August election, would merely cut back the work force in Roanoke Rapids and move much, if not all, of its work to non-union mills in other towns. JP could keep that up indefinitely, unless the union chased JP wherever it went. "They didn't respond," Eli says.

Still, he had planned a rally for that afternoon and that night, urging his staff to round up every available mill hand off work and pack the paperworkers' hall. Perhaps the sight of hundreds of cheering mill hands would move Stettin and Swaity to launch Eli's grand plan. Only twenty workers appeared for the afternoon rally, and Eli knew then that something was wrong. Had his own staff forgotten to make the calls, to spread the word? Or worse, had they quietly ignored him, refusing to turn out a large crowd, turning on Eli because he had pushed them, ridden them, for months?

At the midnight rally, Eli again counted twenty mill hands in the hall. He looked at the workers, standing in front of them, seeing them sit, merely sit quietly, waiting, and then he looked at his staff. "They undercut me. I felt like I'd been knifed," Eli says. He turned to McIver, standing by him with Stettin and Swaity, and as Eli began walking to the door, he told McIver, "I've done what I can do. You've got yourself a winner here." An hour later, in his room at the Motel Dixie, Eli typed his final report. He wrote in the space at the bottom: "With full realization I have contributed all I was capable of to this campaign, in the best interests of all, I leave the campaign."

Afterword

A CROWD OF MILL HANDS, most of them men, stood outside under the lights of the Rosemary mill. It was nearing ten o'clock at night, and the heat of the summer day, August 23, 1974, could still be felt in the blacktop of the street and the concrete of the sidewalk. It was a waiting crowd, so quiet that one mill hand standing in it said to another, "A dog wouldn't bark on a night like this."

The mill hands were outside the central personnel office of J. P. Stevens & Co., Inc., in Roanoke Rapids. The air conditioning inside the building proved too slight to cool the jammed rooms, and for hours the mill hands in the street had been looking through open windows, watching other men inside. There were eighty official observers in the large room that made up one side of the one-story building. Forty of those were mill hands for JP who had joined the union, or members of the union staff. Forty others were bossmen for JP. There were sixteen agents of the National Labor Relations Board inside, about a dozen newspaper and television reporters, and, standing by the reporters, apart from the bossmen and apart from the union men, was Eli Zivkovich.

The first shift at the six JP mills voted when it went to work that morning. The third shift, getting off work at the same time, voted with the first shift, at eight o'clock. The second shift voted in the afternoon, when it went into the mills. Paper ballots were used, and all 3,205 of them were going into two stacks on a long table in the center of the room full of sweating men and women. One pile was votes for the union, the other pile votes against it.

Crystal Lee's ballot was there. It was put in a separate pile with seventy-one others, each ballot challenged by JP because none of those seventy-two mill hands any longer worked for JP. The challenges would be settled in court, if the vote were that close.

Mason Lee and Tommy Gardner, two of Crystal Lee's bossmen, were among the JP observers. Eli looked at the two men as the ballots were stacked. "The agents from the NLRB put them in 'no' and 'yes' piles by hand, and then they were going to count them out. When all the ballots were leveled out on the table, it looked absolutely even," Eli says. "Things were quiet then, and the labor-board people looked like they could see the company had won," he said. Lee and Gardner stood across the table from Eli. "They were frozen-faced," Eli says. "The board may have thought it was a 'no' vote, but I don't think the company did. They knew that this was it. There was no smiling, no talk from that side. We were standing up on chairs to see, workers standing up on chairs to watch the count," he says.

The labor-board agents counted the 'no' ballots, those against the union, first. They ran out of ballots at 1,448. "And that's when the tears of joy began for us," Eli says. The company had 1,448 votes, the union, 1,685. Eli turned from the counting table and pressed through the shouting mill hands to get out the door.

Eli was through here, through with the town and through with the union, he thought. He had come back from curiosity, and at his own expense, to see the results of what he still believed had been his and Crystal Lee's campaign. Now he had only one thing to do before leaving town. He had kept in touch, by phone, with both Crystal Lee and Cookie since their separation in March. Crystal Lee's search for work in Burlington had been fruitless, and after Cookie agreed to leave the house and take an apartment in town, she had returned to Roanoke Rapids, living with the children at 30 Henry Street, waiting around herself, curious, to see first-hand how the campaign ended. Eli had promised Cookie and Crystal Lee that he would see them before leaving town, and he had promised to help Cookie make one more effort at reconciliation.

Eli stayed at a Holiday Inn this time, on the edge of town, a far plusher place than the Motel Dixie. The union staff was there, and outside his motel door the sounds of their victory party could be heard. Mill hands and union organizers laughed and drank by the swimming pool. At eleven o'clock there was a knock on Eli's door. It was Cookie.

The two men talked until four the next morning, and for the first time, Cookie let out his feelings. "My entire married life has not been at all what I wanted it to be. One thing I can say: it hasn't been dull. I can say that. I have never wanted to be a controversial person. I just never wanted to be that way. And it seems more and more as I go on in life, that's happening to me. I'm being drawn into issues that separate everybody. Things just don't go the way that I want them to go. And it seems to me, dammit, some things ought to work the way you want them to work. Some things," he said.

Nothing he wanted, even before he had met Crystal Lee, before she had joined the union, had ever come his way. "I don't know, I just feel like I coulda done a whole lots better than what I done. You listen to people say you create our own opportunity. Dang if I ain't been trying for a long time, and it just don't look like that golden opportunity has knocked on my door. Luck just hasn't been with me the way I would have liked it to be," Cookie said.

He hated what the union campaign had done to him, and to his marriage. Crystal Lee's telling the story of her affairs, of Jay's birth, whatever it might have done for her, had been terrible pain for him. "Because we wanted our names in the headlines? That is why we did it? Brother, let me tell you something: this ain't brought us nothing but one hell to live in. I could have very well done without it. She made a commitment to it. She thought it would help. I thought it would help. I mean, you think about this thing, telling that story and living in this town, some people knew it, some knew it, some thought it. We talked it over, and we just decided, well, it'll hurt us, it'll hurt. But it'll help too. It'll help somebody else," Cookie said.

Just before sunrise, Eli phoned Crystal Lee. He and Cookie were coming over, he said, and they were on the way now. "She met us at the door. And we talked and talked," Eli says. "She looked at him, just telling him, 'Look, you tried to keep me away from this. You denied me my rights.' I remember telling Cookie, 'Well, there it is, Cookie. You can't take it away from this woman.' And you can't."

Eli left Crystal Lee and Cookie soon after dawn. He had his suitcase to pack at the motel, and as he gathered his things in the room, for the first time the import of the election struck him. No major textile chain, not even a single large cotton mill, had been organized and then held anywhere in the South before. No one in JP, nor in the union, had believed the mill hands here wanted a union, no one except Crystal Lee and Eli. That day after the votes were counted, no one in the company, nor in the union, could explain the outcome. For eight years hardly anyone had paid particular attention to the mill hands in Roanoke Rapids. When someone did, things had changed. But not everything.

Eli Zivkovich stood on the sidewalk in front of the union office on Roanoke Avenue. He was ready to get in his car, parked at the curb in front of him, and go home to West Virginia. A young man walked up to him, handed him a letter, turned and walked away without a word. Eli opened the letter. It was from JP, addressed to the union. There were two paragraphs to the letter. The first said the company recognized that the union had finally won an election. JP was ready to bargain, the letter said. But there were mills to run in the meantime, JP said, and "operational decisions and changes arising continually and daily."

JP could not speak for the union, the letter said. But here was one thing the company knew: "It would appear that the only thing to do is for us to continue handling such matters as nearly as possible just as we have been doing heretofore."

Eli took the letter inside the TWUA office. He gave it to an organizer, one he did not recognize. Then he turned around without a word, walked to his car, got in, and drove home.

At 30 Henry Street that morning, Crystal Lee told Cookie for the first time all of the things she did not like in him, all of the things she felt he had done wrong since their marriage. And Cookie told her, "We can work it out." She did not know if they could. She was a different woman now, even Cookie could see that, but what difference would it make? "Cookie had learned to respect me for being the way I am," Crystal Lee says now. "See, I was a daddy's girl. My daddy loved me too much. He did. Too much," she says. Crystal Lee told Cookie she would try. Perhaps, she told herself, they could start all over again.